And also the...

Dedication

---

*To those who have heard or read sections of this
over the last year with patience and wisdom.*

Thank you.

And
Also The
Cucumbers

Anthony Buckley

Highland

First published in 2023 by Highland Books, 1 Fairfield Close, Exmouth, EX8 2BN, England

ISBN-13: 978-1-897913-98-7

ISBN-10: 1-897913-98-2

Ebook ISBN: 978-1-909690-98-1

Printed in the UK by CPI Books

Contents

Phrases from the Prophets

Phrases from the John the Baptist Narrative

Phrases from the Jesus Narrative

Phrases from the Life of the Early Church

Introductory
Thoughts

Words from a wise elf

Counsel for the peril of the world?

In *The Lord of the Rings,* Elrond says:

> *That is the purpose for which you are called
> hither. Called, I say, though I have not called
> you to me, strangers from distant lands. You
> have come and are here met, in this very nick
> of time, by chance as it may seem. Yet it is not
> so. Believe rather that it is so ordered that we,
> who sit here, and none others, must now find
> counsel for the peril for the world.* [1]

We are where we are. We may be pleased that we
are, or we may be wishing we were somewhere else.
But, like it or not, we are where we are. Wherever
that is, we may wonder how we might find counsel
for the perils and joys, small or large, that we face.
And this counsel is needed for the sake of others,
for the world, as well as for ourselves.

The call to find good counsel, to live wisely, is
marbled throughout the Bible. Often it is in clear
guidance, for example in the book of Proverbs.

---

1 "The Lord of the Rings", J. R. R. Tolkien, first volume
   published in 1954. Allen & Unwin

Equally often it is in the narratives, when the reader is implicitly invited to consider the wisdom (or not) of what is being said and done by the characters. This slim volume is a series of reflections on some of these narrative moments. My thanks to the many different groups and churches who have heard earlier versions of some of the examples. The choice of texts may seem slightly random, even idiosyncratic ('This I call to mind'[2] contained other texts, and thanks are due to kind and patient readers who encouraged another book with this format).

It is reported that Winston Churchill once said about a political adversary: *Occasionally he stumbled over the truth, but hastily picked himself up and hurried on as if nothing had happened.* Sometimes the wisdom that is present in narratives is ignored as we scamper through to the end. Central to being wise is the willingness to attend to wisdom, to be alert and watchful, to be asking: What can I learn from this incident, phrase, song or letter? Wisdom may be found in unexpected places: *All scripture,* writes Paul, *is God-breathed and is useful for teaching, rebuking, correcting and training in righteousness, so that the servant of God may be thoroughly equipped for every good work.* All scripture, even a grumble about cucumbers.

---

2   "This I call to mind", A. G. Buckley. 2017, Highland Books

Much of what we now find in the Bible would have been first heard rather than read: sitting round the campfire or crowded in a meeting, hidden in a room or in a cave, in a synagogue or convent, kitchen table or monastery, or in a church whilst wondering if the weather would hold for a good harvest. Quietly read or loudly declaimed as the context demanded. Or indeed hearing it for the fifteenth time, valuing the familiar whilst relishing the skill of the reader as the tale is told anew. A hand would sometimes have gone up, or a head lifted with a searching gaze. Some of these would have been feisty gatherings: *I don't understand / don't agree / That's it! / Yes, but...* There may have been an uncomfortable shifting as the challenge hit home, or sometimes an inward smile of comfort or relief. One or two of the phrases may have caused a smile and a rolling of the eyes. Some may have caused tears.

There is a danger in a book such as this. Can we be sure that the thoughts offered are part of the witness of scripture or might they only be self-indulgent projections by the author? And of course, this has been one of the callings of the church through history, to discuss and weigh interpretations that are offered. So please sit lightly on my thoughts.

Believe rather that it is so ordered that we,
who sit here, and none others, must now find
counsel for the peril for the world

The calling to seek wisdom, counsel for the peril of the world, is a great privilege. Wisdom might be defined as: Seeking to understand, as best we can, how the world is, and how to live well within it. As we explore something about the nature and workings of God (if we are a person of faith), of others and ourselves, as we sit round the metaphorical campfire, hearing these ancient narratives, may we be granted humility and anticipation, and a desire to put to good use whatever we may hear.

We are where we are. And perhaps we may note the words of St Paul, so poignantly aware of his past, to the Corinthians: *By the grace of God I am what I am, and his grace to me was not without effect.*

Likewise with us, always. His grace is not without effect.

– 1 –

Queen Esther

For such a time as this
Esther 4:14

"Where are you?" is the first question God asks in the Bible. Where we are, our place, condition, and context, matter. We begin with an assurance and challenge to the young Queen Esther, who had to face (probably in the fifth century BC) the fact that, whether she liked it or not, she was where she was. She needed good counsel, and she needed it quickly.

In Esther chapter 4 we read:

> When Esther's words were reported to
> Mordecai, he sent back this answer: "Do not
> think that because you are in the king's house
> you alone of all the Jews will escape. For if
> you remain silent at this time, relief and
> deliverance for the Jews will arise from another
> place, but you and your father's family will
> perish. And who knows but that you have
> come to your royal position for such a time as
> this?"

For such a time as this, there's the challenge.

> *Then Esther sent this reply to Mordecai: "Go, gather together all the Jews who are in Susa, and fast for me. Do not eat or drink for three days, night or day. I and my attendants will fast as you do. When this is done, I will go to the king, even though it is against the law. And if I perish, I perish."*

Esther had not expected to become Queen. King Xerxes had decided he needed a new wife after his desire to humiliate Queen Vashti by parading her in front of his over-partied nobles had been frustrated by her refusal. Vashti comes out of the account with self-respect intact, Xerxes does not. It is one of those feasts in the Bible when too much drink and showing off mean the evening does not end well...

The journey towards Esther being Queen had thus been complicated and unexpected. But now she was where she was, for such a time as this. The implication for the listeners is clear. Wherever we are, however we have got there, whether through careful planning or through the failings of others or of ourselves, we can dare to trust that there is a purpose for us.

There would have been the temptation to do nothing. Her people, the Jews, in exile, were facing a new and severe persecution, set in train by Xerxes' advisor Haman. But Esther herself was possibly safe. Her guardian, Mordecai, warns her of the perils of staying silent. She must not presume her present comfort is the priority, nor that it will guarantee security. There is also a risk to Mordecai, he must have been very proud that his ward had done so well and would have been desperate to keep her safe. Why suggest she do anything different? But he believed, and Esther believed, that the cause was much bigger.

It was an offence, punishable by death, to go into the king's presence without being summoned. The king could suspend this punishment and show his favour if he held his gold sceptre to the uninvited supplicant. It was a risk, and Esther takes the risk, having sent a message to Mordecai to ask her people to be fasting for her. It is a moment of genuine tension as she enters the king's hall, and we are then told *he was pleased with her and held out to her the gold sceptre that was in his hand.*

And who knows but that you have come to your royal position for such a time as this?

Inspirational words across the centuries to so many who have heard this story, and have understood that the adjective 'royal' can be widely interpreted. Esther's trust, courage and reliance on friends have been much noted by those seeking wisdom.

Back to Elrond: *You have come and are here met, in this very nick of time, by chance as it may seem. Yet it is not so. Believe rather that*

it is so ordered that we, who sit here, and none
others, must now find counsel for the peril for
the world.

These words provide a pivotal moment in 'The Lord of the Rings'. Here is a quiet assertion that there is a higher power at work, that things don't happen by accident, that there is a force for good operating out of immediate sight. Perhaps this helps give confidence to the characters, giving a sense of purpose to their desire to seek counsel for the perils they face.

For reflection

- How well do we understand our sense of calling?

- How can we wisely make the most of where we are?

− 2 −

A different league table

> *He was wiser than anyone else,*
> *including Ethan the Ezrahite*
> *1 Kings 4:31*

An older narrative than the story of Esther is that of Solomon. Ethan the Ezrahite... beaten into second place.

Wisdom mattered to King Solomon. Knowing he was going to become king after David, he had prayed for wisdom, and the prayer was granted. The chronicler explains:

> *God gave Solomon wisdom and very great*
> *insight, and a breadth of understanding*
> *as measureless as the sand on the seashore.*
> *Solomon's wisdom was greater than the*
> *wisdom of all the people of the East, and*
> *greater than all the wisdom of Egypt. He was*
> *wiser than anyone else, including Ethan the*
> *Ezrahite − wiser than Heman, Kalkol and*
> *Darda, the sons of Mahol. And his fame spread*
> *to all the surrounding nations. He spoke three*
> *thousand proverbs and his songs numbered*
> *a thousand and five. He spoke about plant*

*life, from the cedar of Lebanon to the hyssop
that grows out of walls. He also spoke about
animals and birds, reptiles and fish. From
all nations people came to listen to Solomon's
wisdom, sent by all the kings of the world, who
had heard of his wisdom.*

There seems to have been some sort of league table
for wisdom, and the writer wanted to be clear that
his king had won. The ranking may feel strange
to our ears, perhaps verging on the arrogant,
but different criteria for leaders have been used
by historians, propagandists and commentators
over the centuries, and the choice of wisdom as
a criterion is, to say the least, less harmful than
some.

Wisdom was clearly a much-valued quality,
and it continued to be so. Nick Page highlights
that this attitude was still present many centuries
later in the time of Christ when people were
weighing up their leaders *Although they valued
family history and breeding to some extent, money
wasn't as important as wisdom.*[3]

As we seek to find wise counsel, the facets of
wisdom the narrator wishes to emphasise may
be noted. One theme is widespread curiosity:
Solomon was interested in trees and reptiles, fish
and plants – the whole natural order. No doubt
his supporters would insist he was a master
in all these fields; we may not feel that we are

3   "The Longest Week", Nick Page, 2009, Hodder and
         Stoughton

similarly blessed, but we note that wisdom here is deliberately marked as different from over-narrow expertise. One gets the impression that Solomon was not easily bored. The writer implies that wisdom includes curiosity, seeking *a breadth of understanding as measureless as the sand as the seashore.*

Another theme is the breadth of creativity through which wisdom is expressed: proverbs, short sayings to show understanding of the world and to make the reader think, the listeners may have been expecting; they might not have been expecting songs, let alone a thousand and five of them. Wisdom can be found in all kinds of media, across all creativity: in paintings and poems, drama and dance, cooking and gardening.

Wisdom needs to be kept fresh. If people are travelling far to listen, then past glories, a perceptive proverb or two ten years ago, will not be enough. Wisdom needs to be in the present, and thus is a quality continually to be nurtured. We all have our different ways of staying wise, be it reading or discussion, reflection or creating; the challenge is to keep attentive, otherwise the Queen of Sheba herself would later not have *come to Solomon and talked with him about all that she had on her mind.* The question may be arising in the listeners' minds: 'How do I keep my wisdom fresh?'

The narrator sees wisdom as a gift from God; this acknowledgement ensures it will be used with humility, gratitude and appreciation.

We may smile at the ranking, but perhaps there are much more destructive league tables for leaders to have in the back of their minds as they run their countries or organisations. What do we look for in our leaders? And in ourselves as we exercise leadership? What priority is given to wisdom?

And no doubt Ethan the Ezrahite was wise enough to smile at this account; he is included elsewhere in the scriptures, as the writer of Psalm 89.

For reflection

- What does wisdom look like when we see it in others or in ourselves?

- How would we feel if we were Ethan the Ezrahite?

— 3 —

Not everyone

wants wisdom

Since you refuse to listen when I call
Proverbs 1:24

The offer of wisdom is sometimes refused. It is not always a treasured quality, nor inevitably absorbed from upbringing, culture or background. As we imagine this sentence being read around the fire, across the supper table or in more formal places, we may wonder what tone would have been used. Was it plaintive or challenging, quiet or robust? And might a particular word be emphasised by the speaker, and, if so, which one? At whom was he or she looking…?

Since you refuse to listen when I call. The 'I' who is calling is Wisdom. The book of Proverbs is one of the five 'wisdom books' of the Old Testament: Job, Psalms, Proverbs, Ecclesiastes, Song of Songs. The opening of Proverbs is an affirmation of the value of wisdom, and explains that the author/ editor will be offering thoughtful sayings:

For receiving instruction in prudent behaviour,
doing what is right and just and fair; for
giving prudence to those who are simple,
knowledge and discretion to the young – let the
wise listen and add to their learning, and let
the discerning get guidance.

Whoever we are, however young or old we are, we can learn wisdom (*simple* in the extract above is better translated as gullible, easily led astray).

Further on, wisdom is personified – *She raises her voice in the public square.*

Shortly after, we have her damning phrase: *You refuse to listen when I call.*

Which word strikes most, whose eye did the narrator wish to catch? Is the emphasis on the *you*? Is this personal? Or do we sometimes *refuse* to hear wisdom's voice? Do we know our inner motives well enough to know whether we want to be wise or not? We might be worried that wisdom will get in the way of what we want to do; perhaps we want the quick victory instead of handling relationships thoughtfully and gently, the fiery soundbite rather than the serious explanation, the formulaic rather than the searching.

The challenge may be that we don't really want to *listen*; we may hear or read many wise thoughts, but do we engage, are we prepared to be changed? When was the last time we heard something we knew to be helpful, and, as a result, altered our behaviour?

Perhaps some listeners hold to the promise in the last three words: *When I call.* Wisdom is calling to us, she is raising her voice in the public square: there can be guidance and clarity, there can be a way forward. Wisdom is continually offered. If we respond we will not be bereft. We will be led safely through.

However people react, however this phrase is read or heard, the encouragement is being given to consider the rich variety of sayings and images that follow in the book of Proverbs. And the underlying challenge is made explicit: not to take for granted that we are automatically wise.

When wisdom calls in the marketplace, who is listening?

For reflection

- How much is wisdom valued in our community and society?

- And in our own lives?

Introductory Thoughts

— 4 —
The foolishness of
the self-important

Who is this son of Jesse?
1 Samuel 25:10

Before Esther, before the book of Proverbs, there was a man called Nabal, rich and successful, owning large flocks. He had been fortunate, his shepherds well-treated by David (at this point not yet king, and in the wilderness). In the eyes of the culture of the time, he had married well.

But these attributes seemed to have brought a spirit of arrogance and entitlement rather than gratitude and generosity.

> *A certain man in Maon, who had property*
> *there at Carmel, was very wealthy. He had*
> *a thousand goats and three thousand sheep,*
> *which he was shearing in Carmel. His name*
> *was Nabal and his wife's name was Abigail.*
> *She was an intelligent and beautiful woman,*
> *but her husband was surly and mean in his*
> *dealings.*

David sends messages asking for help; Nabal is contemptuous, suspicious and miserly.

> *Nabal answered David's servants, "Who is*
> *this David? Who is this son of Jesse? Many*
> *servants are breaking away from their masters*
> *these days. Why should I take my bread and*
> *water, and the meat I have slaughtered for my*
> *shearers, and give it to men coming from who*
> *knows where?"*

This does not end well for Nabal. It will not be
long before he learns, from his wife Abigail, who
this David is, and of what he might be capable.
She waits until the cold light of day to tell him.

> *When Abigail went to Nabal, he was in the*
> *house holding a banquet like that of a king.*
> *He was in high spirits and very drunk. So she*
> *told him nothing at all until daybreak. Then*
> *in the morning, when Nabal was sober, his*
> *wife told him all these things, and his heart*
> *failed him and he became like a stone.*

Ten days later he dies.

Humankind cannot bear very much reality, wrote
T.S. Eliot[4]. The further away we are from reality,
the more difficult it is to bear when we are faced
by it. Nabal was unwise in his meanness, in his
self-importance (*Like that of a king* is a revealing
phrase) and in his contempt. Perhaps he felt he
was so successful that he was invulnerable. The
shock of the truth was too much for him.

Was part of Nabal's foolishness a steady
weaving of an internal narrative which caused him

---

4   "Four Quartets" T. S Eliot, 1941, Faber and Faber

not to care very much what was going on except in his world? David was in the wilderness at this time, but he was a well-known figure at King Saul's court and throughout the country (This was after the dramatic killing of Goliath). Why was Nabal not more emotionally sensitive to what this request might signify, and from whom it came?

But, as ever, it is all too easy to look for the Nabal in others, and not in ourselves. This is not a moment to be smug. The wise know that the frailties of others can be seen or exceeded in themselves.

And, just to provide a further twist, David ends up marrying Abigail.

For reflection

- What is the danger of a sense of entitlement?

- How can we guard against it?

Phrases from the
Moses Narrative

– 5 –

Asking the right question
___

> *Shall I go and get one of the Hebrew*
> *women to nurse the baby for you?*
> *Exodus 2:7*

Wisdom is sometimes about knowing the context well enough to ask the right question at the right time.

Nabal, Abigail, David, Solomon and contemporaries would have known the earlier great narratives, including the story of Moses, and we turn briefly there.

The older sister, seeing that her baby brother floating down the Nile had been picked up by Pharaoh's daughter, intervenes to keep the narrative moving in the right direction. She presumably had perceived the compassion in the actions of the princess (who clearly did not agree with her father's command that all Hebrew baby boys should be killed). Moses' sister's question was helpful, non-threatening, well-timed and strategic; it was received well. It is a great gift to ask the right question well. She goes to fetch one of the Hebrew women, who just happens to be her mother. This would involve a sacrifice, she would be partially losing her mother to the palace. But she loved her brother (what had she felt as she had stayed watching the basket float down the Nile?) and her family, and this must have seemed a good result.

Moses himself, when older, is not so perceptive, strategic or timely when he asks someone, "*Why are you hitting your fellow Hebrew?*" The reply is swift and blunt: "*Who made you ruler and judge over us? Are you thinking of killing me as you killed the Egyptian?*" Moses was assuming an authority which he had not been given; his violence the previous day makes his present question look hypocritical. His assertiveness and timing land badly. He flees from Egypt.

Perhaps he still feels the pain of that taunting question when, after years in the wilderness, he responds to an unexpected calling to return and rescue his people: *Who am I, that I should go to Pharaoh and bring the Israelites out of Egypt?* Perhaps on his mind was that past failure all those years ago, when he had got the timing and the wording wrong. A more explicit excuse is offered a few verses later when he says he has difficulties with his speech. Or perhaps there was simply that understandable fear of the enormity of the task. *Who am I to do such a thing as this?* It is a very human question, and unconsciously or consciously is often asked.

The divine answer is simple: "I will be with you." Although Moses does not quite know it yet, that is all he needed to hear.

And then, the crucial question that he asks of God,

> *"Suppose I go to the Israelites and say to them,*
> *'The God of your fathers has sent me to you,'*
> *and they ask me, 'What is his name?' Then*
> *what shall I tell them?"*

It is the right question: we need to be wise as to who is sending us, what is driving us and what is the authority behind us.

And the rest, as they say, is history.

Moses' older sister asked the right questions; in time, so did he. For those of us who have used the wrong words, made the wrong challenge, in the past, may Moses' story be an encouragement. And may we learn from the skill of his sister.

For reflection

- What helps us to ask good questions, that can keep the conversation growing, that can keep the narrative moving?

— 6 —

Not always making a fuss

Also the cucumbers
Numbers 11:5

After a series of extraordinary events, Moses leads his people out of slavery in Egypt and begins the journey to the Promised Land, nourished by manna. But there is murmuring...

> *The rabble with them began to crave other food, and again the Israelites started wailing and said, "If only we had meat to eat! We remember the fish we ate in Egypt at no cost — also the cucumbers, melons, leeks, onions and garlic. But now we have lost our appetite; we never see anything but this manna!"*

They were not in desperate straits, food was being provided. But they are becoming bored with manna, divine blessing though it is. There then follows a slightly defensive explanatory comment from the narrator about the delights of manna (his description of the people as 'the rabble' makes it clear where he stands).

*The manna was like coriander seed and looked
like resin. The people went around gathering
it, and then ground it in a hand-mill or
crushed it in a mortar. They cooked it in a
pot or made it into loaves. And it tasted like
something made with olive oil.*

The manna was more than adequate and was clearly
versatile. It could be cooked or baked and seemed
flavoured with a hint of olive oil: not bad, one would
have thought, for nourishment provided free and
easily available on a wilderness journey, and with the
cheerful hope of the Promised Land lying ahead.

But we find it difficult to be content. We
remember the cucumbers. And all those other things
which, looking back from a point of relative need,
are remembered as being so, so good, so much better
than the gifts in the present situation. But in truth,
in Egypt the cucumbers had been rather tainted by
the suffering, the slavery and the killing; perhaps
they had not been enjoyed quite as much as was now
recalled. Our memories can play tricks.

And Moses then has to work out how he can
keep this large and frequently complaining group
moving forward. He prays robustly and the outcome
is that quail is sent alongside the manna. There is a
graciousness in the workings of God. He gives more
than is needed, perhaps partly because we do not
quite know what we really need, and can grumble or
panic easily.

Sometimes we have already made our point, but
we wish to pile on superfluous layers of argument.

The people had talked about the lack of fish but were not sure that the case had been firmly enough made. And so they raise the stakes and mention the cucumbers. And then the melons... and on it goes. Did they really think that Moses would say to himself "They are even grieving the onions, this must be really serious?" Knowing the level of fuss that is worth making, and when to stop, is another sign of wisdom.

It all sounds slightly ridiculous but may quietly strike a chord and the lesson is not pressed too hard. No doubt one or two pairs of eyes roll when, many years later, the narrator put on a wistful or moaning voice and said: "Also the cucumbers...?"

But did one or two of the listeners wonder if they would have made the same complaint?

When we venture back into the past we are not going back to how it was, but how we now think it was. There needs to be a cool-headedness and humility about the joys and the sorrows we may be assuming we are finding there. And if yesterday's memories cause us to downplay today's blessings and tomorrow's hope, then we should be especially wary.

For reflection

- Do we know when to pause in our list of complaints?

- How best can we check if we are remembering well?

– 7 –

An old man on a hill

With the staff of God in my hands
Exodus 17:9

The Exodus story continues; Moses and the Israelites draw closer to the Promised Land, but there is a struggle ahead. Moses explains his plan:

Tomorrow I will stand on top of the hill with the staff of God in my hands

Moses has told Joshua, *Choose some of our men and go out to fight the Amalekites.* Those listening may have wondered why Moses is not going to be in the battle, would it not be more useful to use the staff of God to hit Amalekites over the head? (The modern reader may have images of Gandalf doing likewise in 'The Lord of the Rings' – except, perhaps significantly, those moments only happen in the films, not in the original book; in the book the staff is used powerfully, but never violently)

Moses trusts Joshua. The younger man can be entrusted with the battle, the skill of delegation is often highlighted in these Old Testament narratives. That in itself may have caused listeners to think, and it is a theme that is returned to in the next chapter. But for the moment the narrative continues:

> So Joshua fought the Amalekites as Moses had ordered, and Moses, Aaron and Hur went to the top of the hill. As long as Moses held up his hands, the Israelites were winning, but whenever he lowered his hands, the Amalekites were winning. When Moses' hands grew tired, they took a stone and put it under him and he sat on it. Aaron and Hur held his hands up — one on one side, one on the other — so that his hands remained steady till sunset. So Joshua overcame the Amalekite army with the sword.

In that culture, holding up one's hands was a sign that one was praying. The message is clear, it was prayer that was winning the battle. But the narrative develops further: There is an understanding that we can become tired; if we are no longer able to stand all day, then it is fine to sit. That however weary we may feel, our day is not past (Moses' role is as significant as ever, just different). That we need friends who will help us and who will stay with us. That we can sometimes be a friend to someone else, and keep their hands held high. That Moses keeps going…

Perhaps people heard the phrase and wondered: When I face my daily struggle today, will there be someone on the hill praying for me? Or who is the person fighting their particular battle, for whom I can be praying? Where is the place of prayer in our understanding of wisdom?

In my first Bible there were some colour pictures. Out of all the possible images of the countless stories and events that could have been chosen, a depiction of this episode was included, perhaps it struck the picture-editor as much as it may have done to those first listeners, all those years ago: The old man on the hill, his life full of triumphs and failures, keeping hold of the staff of God. He will keep praying. The courage and persistence to pray when there may be voices suggesting there is no need, or that we should be doing other things, is a sign of a life wisely lived.

For reflection

- What tempts us to forget the importance of prayer?

— 8 —

The wisdom of
taking advice

___

What you are doing is not good
Exodus 18:17

As the Moses narrative continued, this phrase may have caused a raised eyebrow or two among the listeners round the circle.

> *Moses' father-in-law replied, 'What you are doing is not good. You and these people who come to you will only wear yourselves out. The work is too heavy for you; you cannot handle it alone.*

As some of a certain age may know, Jethro Tull was a pop group formed in the 1960s, named after Jethro Tull, a key figure in the British Agricultural Revolution who, in 1700, invented his innovative horse-pulled seed drill. He would have been named after another Jethro (in those days people knew their Bibles well), and this Jethro had a part to play in the great narrative of the Old Testament, because he was the father-in-law of Moses.

There is much that could be said about Jethro, but here we focus on a moment when he meets Moses and asks how things are going. Moses tells his father-in law the great story of the Liberation and Exodus from Egypt. Jethro *was delighted to hear about all the good things.*

But the next day we have: *What you are doing is not good.*

This is Jethro, talking to his son-in-law. Criticism within families, especially between in-laws, does not always land well. Jethro says it, anyway. He is talking to Moses – *The* Moses, the great leader, through whom God has already done so much. Jethro says it, anyway. Many years before, Jethro had employed Moses, and so perhaps he was used to the mixed roles.

What you are doing is not good.

The context is this, Moses is sitting in judgement on all the disputes and queries that are on his people's minds. Jethro sees the dangers, but knows it is never particularly helpful for someone to criticise without suggesting a way through, and he avoids that trap.

> *Select capable men from all the people – men who fear God, trustworthy men who hate dishonest gain – and appoint them as officials over thousands, hundreds, fifties and tens. Let them serve as judges for the people at all times, but let them bring every difficult case to you; the simple cases they can decide themselves.*

> *That will make your load lighter, because*
> *they will share it with you. If you do this and*
> *God so commands, you will be able to stand*
> *the strain, and all these people will go home*
> *satisfied.*

We do not know how Jethro said the criticising phrase, the tone of voice matters so much when we need to correct. He had been fulsome in his praise the day before, recognising all that was good that had happened; criticism is more likely to land well when it is the context of affirmation. Delegation is an important issue and Jethro, despite the relationship, despite Moses' high status, had the courage to speak.

Moses had the grace to accept it.

Those who told and re-told this story included this exchange. We can think of people, perhaps even ourselves, who would have wanted to influence the re-telling of this narrative: 'I realised I could do this in an even a better way, I am very collaborative and so I ran it past Jethro. And then I brought in a new system.' But the storytellers did not soften it, they included this section without comment, and the listeners then decide to make of it what they will. Moses' status and esteem did not suffer from his willingness to accept advice.

> *You will be able to stand the strain, and all*
> *these people will go home satisfied.*

In modern parlance, that would be called a win-win!

For reflection
- How best can we receive and give advice?

Phrases from the
Psalms

— 9 —

Mulling things over

> *These are the things I go over and over*
> *Psalm 42:4*

We may remember from an earlier chapter that one expression of wisdom was writing songs. There are songs throughout the Bible; the longest collection is found in the book of Psalms. Singing psalms was part of the narrative of the people of Israel, it was a communal activity, shaping the community in the sharing of the remembrances, the doubts, hopes and joys.

Here are two translations (*New International Version* and *The Message*) of Psalm 42, verse 4

> *These things I remember as I pour out my soul:*
> *how I used to go to the house of God under the*
> *protection of the Mighty One, with shouts of*
> *joy and praise among the festive throng.*

> *These are the things I go over and over,*
> *emptying out the pockets of my life.*
> *I was always at the head of the worshiping*
> *crowd, right out in front,*

Leading them all, eager to arrive and worship,
Shouting praises, singing thanksgiving—
celebrating, all of us, God's feast!

But life does not feel so good now.

Psalm 42, along with Psalm 43, repeats variations of the despondent refrain: *Why my soul, are you downcast?* In verse 4 the psalmist calls to mind the days that were good, but seems in other verses to be trying to work out how they fit in the current bleak season: *Why my soul, are you downcast? Why so disturbed within me? – I say to my God my Rock, "Why have you forgotten me?"*

The writer is glad that there were times when he was part of something celebratory, larger and full of faith. He is thankful that they happened, that he was there; it feels good to call them to mind, however wistfully. We note the honesty of the psalmist, and of the later editors who kept this psalm in the collection; appropriate poignancy can be an important part of our worship and wisdom.

The psalmist deliberately writes an internally contradictory line: *I say to my God my Rock, "Why have you forgotten me?"* How can someone rock-like in their reliability be forgetful? – Did the singers give a wry smile as they sang this couplet? Perhaps there is insight here – sometimes our feelings and faith may not seem quite to fit together, and the psalmist has caught this very human tendency to be tangled and contradictory.

The psalm reminds of the importance of being together. The psalmist liked celebrating with others: walking, joking, sharing old stories, singing. He currently is no longer in that place, physically, mentally or spiritually (perhaps all three), but holds on to what was important for him, then.

And will be again. In the memories lie the foundation of his hope. A theme throughout the psalms (and indeed throughout the scriptures) is that all that is good is of God, and therefore cannot be lost, however much it may disappear from our limited vision. It belongs to his eternal time, not within created linear time. The verse is not simply nostalgia, it is indeed a re-membering, a bringing back together of important and shaping experiences.

Verse 5 holds the balance: honesty about the present, assurance for the future.

> *Why, my soul, are you downcast? Why so*
> *disturbed within me?*
> *Put your hope in God, for I will yet praise*
> *him, my Saviour and my God.*

These are the things I go over and over.

For reflection

- How, and why, do *we go over and over* certain things in our past?

- What questions are we truly prepared to ask about ourselves and our stories?

- Where do we find our hope?

— 10 —

Where a tree needs to be

Like a tree planted by streams of water
Psalm 1

Most of us have the desire to be of some use, to make a difference, to be fruitful. The psalm chosen to open the collection which has become the oldest continuously used song book in history begins:

> *Blessed is the one who*
> *does not walk in step with the wicked*
> *or stand in the way that sinners take*
> *or sit in the company of mockers,*
> *but whose delight is in the law of the Lord,*
> *and who meditates on his law day and night.*
> *That person is like a tree planted*
> *by streams of water,*
> *which yields its fruit in season*

When the tree is in the right place, it will flourish. The right place, for the psalmist, is in the intentional avoidance of destructive behaviour and unkind words; it is in the dwelling on, discussing and learning about, the wisdom of God, as expressed in the narratives and teachings surrounding the history of God's relationship with his people.

And then the fruit will come. We may need to be patient, but at the right time the flourishing will be evident, in due season. We note that the imagery is of streams, not a pond; there is something refreshing, lively and ongoing in our calling to delight in what is good.

But it can be rather tempting to walk in step with the wicked, and to join our voices with the cynical and scornful. Psalms were written for the community, knowing that we often need each other's help and guidance to navigate the choices we make. If ever we read a psalm on our own, it can be helpful to read it aloud, and to imagine other voices joining in. We are part of the community of God's people, however we might be feeling this day. We always are praying together.

When Jesus says his disciples should pray *Our* Father, a similar point is being made.

For reflection

- What can deflect us from wanting to live wise and good lives?

- And what can encourage us?

— 11 —

We do not always have
to be saving the world

I have calmed and quietened myself
Psalm 131

Psalm 131 is one of the 'Songs of Ascent', sung as people walked up to the Temple in Jerusalem. Songs of memory, assurance and even triumph. And amongst them we have this psalm, and these words.

> *I do not concern myself with great matters*
> *or things too wonderful for me. But I have*
> *calmed and quieted myself, I am like a weaned*
> *child with its mother; like a weaned child I*
> *am content.*

The theme seems out of place: this is the people of God who are called to be a beacon to the world, but now are singing about the wisdom of switching off for a time. The psalm is comforting or challenging, depending on the personality or mood of the listener. There are times when we might be delighted to do nothing else except relax in our own limitations; there may be other times when we find it frustrating not to be solving every problem that springs to mind, when our mind is full of grandiose hopes and plans.

This is not a private psalm, although it feels personal and intimate, this is for public proclamation, for communal singing. The writer and later compilers must have felt that it was a sign of wisdom to know when to calm down, to step back from the soap box, to be quiet and secure. We really don't always need to be throwing our weight around. The writers knew very well that there are times when we are called to stretch ourselves, to think wide and high and deep, but equally knew that a balance needs to be struck, and hence Psalm 131 is included.

The words are reminiscent of the passage in Ecclesiastes chapter 3, *For everything there is a season, and a time for every matter under heaven.*

In the 1662 Prayer Book of the Church of England we are encouraged to pray for the King *that under him we may be godly and quietly governed.* The word *quietly* is intentional; we need leaders who can run a smooth ship as well as an exciting one (and it often takes much more skill to do so).

The psalm begins: *My heart is not proud, Lord, my eyes are not haughty.* Sometimes the uncomfortable truth is that we want to involve ourselves with events above our experience or expertise; we feel our voice must be heard, and louder than anyone else's. And of course sadly we sometimes are tempted to comment on other people's affairs, even when we have little knowledge or understanding. Perhaps *things too wonderful for me* covers a wide range of topics.

The child, used as an image, knows he or she is nourished and content, is well-looked after, is trusting that all is in hand, that all shall be well. There is no need to be over-interfering in our neighbour's business.

For reflection

- How often do we allow ourselves to be childlike, and to lay aside the big issues for a time?

– 12 –

The wisdom of not
losing control

Dashes them against the rocks
Psalm 137

Sometimes the angry message is kept in drafts and then deleted in the clearer light of the new morning. Sometimes, after due reflection, a version is sent. One of the noticeable features of the psalms is that there are several such angry moments, but they are not deleted. They were intentionally included, not as an example to follow but as a warning to heed, and always as an encouragement to be honest about our feelings. They do not get much more challenging than the sentiments at the end of Psalm 137. The opening is poignant and beautiful: How indeed do we sing the Lord's song in a strange land? What is it like to be a people in exile, by the waters of Babylon? And these themes would be worth considering deeply as the listeners seek wisdom, but our focus now is on the difficult words at the end:

> *Daughter Babylon, doomed to destruction,*
> *happy is the one who repays you according*
> *to what you have done to us. Happy is the*
> *one who seizes your infants and dashes them*
> *against the rocks.*

Let us note that these words would have been as shocking when first read as they are now. It is an avoidance of the issue, and historically untrue, simply to say, "We live in more enlightened times." These words would have been appalling then and they are appalling now.

But the psalmist and the editors left them in. Why? We cannot be certain, and one feature of the scriptures is that nearly always the compilers trust the readers to engage and question and debate and try to work things out for themselves. We are not to be spoon-fed – we have to do the hard thinking. What can we learn from these words? Why were they kept in?

Perhaps these verses hold up a mirror to our secret anger, prejudice and contempt. We may keep these politely under wraps, but the psalmist, with customary openness, forces us to ask whether we are not quite so loving to our enemies as we pretend to be. Have we ever secretly rejoiced when an enemy tripped up in some way? Have we allowed revenge to fester and grow inside us? The psalm is a terrible and extreme reminder of what can happen when we allow hate to take over.

Secondly, if we change roles, if we imagine ourselves to be the Babylonians, the psalm reminds us that if we oppress and mistreat others, if we manipulate and exploit, then we may cause untold spiritual harm as they nurse their injuries and their grudges. Have we ever driven someone to have such awful feelings? Do we ever push someone into a corner so all they can do is turn and snap?

Thirdly, we do not need to hide our thoughts from God. As the ancient prayer has it: *Almighty God, from whom no secrets are hid*, so let's not pretend. A wonderful feature of the psalms is the honesty, although sometimes it may be embarrassing to hear, sometimes even embarrassing to say, sometimes even embarrassing to know we might be thinking it. The psalmist knew that God was able to handle our anger.

St Paul was to write that one purpose of the scriptures was to remind us of our need of salvation; Psalm 137 unpleasantly but deliberately reminds us of that need. Very sadly as we look round our world, we see that same need, and as we look through history, we see that same need. St James was to say that the scriptures are like a mirror. Mirrors are not always fun, especially first thing in the morning, but we are probably glad if we see something that needs checking.

As the listeners sought wisdom in this psalm, they may have sensed the challenge of the need to learn how to handle such strong feelings.

For reflection

- How do we handle our vengeful thoughts?
- How can we avoid pushing someone so hard that they find it difficult to respond well?

— 13 —

Valuing the music

in the chaos

Praise him with the strings and pipe
Psalm 150

Praise the Lord.
Praise God in his sanctuary;
praise him in his mighty heavens.

Praise him for his acts of power;
praise him
for his surpassing greatness.

Praise him
with the sounding of the trumpet,
praise him
with the harp and lyre,

Praise him
with tambourine and dancing,
praise him
with the strings and pipe,

*Praise him
with the clash of cymbals,
praise him
with resounding cymbals.*

*Let everything that has breath
praise the Lord.*

Praise the Lord.

The final song in the book of Psalms is a command to praise. This may feel all very well when we are feeling good and the sun is shining, but it may jar when the weather is bad.

And perhaps it is meant to fit into both contexts, to comfort and to challenge.

This psalm is not designed to stop people weeping when it is right for them to weep, it is not meant to side-line emotional distress. The psalms are full of laments. Jesus himself wept at the tomb of Lazarus, there are times when sadness needs to be recognised and honoured.

The placing it at the end of this collection of greatly varying emotions is a reminder that 'The world is all mixed up, as we have seen in the last 149 psalms, but yet…'

The world is as it is, but yet… The editorial choice of this psalm to finish the book is a challenge. It reminds us that our capacity and calling to praise do not rely on feelings or circumstances. There are echoes in Paul's command to be thankful *in all circumstances*. Centuries earlier than Paul,

Habakkuk would remind us that even when the fig tree is not bearing fruit, yet we can still rejoice in God. In the midst of all we are going through, there will always be something for which we can be grateful. Yes, even in this darkness, hand me the cymbal, or the lyre.

The psalm focuses on God's character and works, it does not suggest bland and unfocused praise. Whatever is happening, the psalmist is trusting in a God who has proved his faithfulness. We may do this through gritted teeth (as many of the psalms do) or in times of great joy; either way, the psalmist wants to hold in mind the unchanging nature of God.

We are reminded that our differences are a blessing. The psalm does not envisage a one-man band. There will be gifted lyre players alongside gifted pipe players. And even the variety of cymbal players is acknowledged.

It is all rather chaotic. How can this end up being a nice and organised sound? But that does not seem to be a priority. We may even think that some instruments are superfluous, but somehow the conductor feels they are all needed.

For reflection

- How well do we handle variety?

- And a little bit of chaos…?

Phrases from the
Prophets

— 14 —

Justice matters

I despise your religious festivals
Amos 5:21

When this was first read, might there have been
not only a startled looking up but even a rush for
the exits, either because of affronted pride or from
shame and anguish (or fear)?

The words of the prophets were as much
part of the narrative as were the songs of the
psalmists; these were the voices of a rich variety
of individuals speaking from the edges of power.
Often dramatically, and with intense imagery, they
would challenge the people, and especially the
rulers, with calls to justice, judgement, assurance
and hope, seeking to bring the word of God into
today's news.

The prophet Amos, a shepherd from Tekoa,
was accustomed to speaking plainly: *Hear this*
word, you cows of Bashan on Mount Samaria, may
already have caused some sharp intakes of breath.

Phrases from the Prophets

Perhaps there were not many left still listening in the market-square by the time this passage was reached:

> *Woe to you who long for the day of the Lord!*
> *Why do you long for the day of the Lord? That*
> *day will be darkness, not light. It will be as*
> *though a man fled from a lion only to meet a*
> *bear...*

There is always the temptation to think justice is on our side, that we are the only ones who really know what is going on, that one day we will be shown to be right. Amos reminds us that on "The Day of the Lord" it will be God, not us, deciding justice.

It is a humbling reminder that we may not always have a complete grasp of the whole story, that we sometimes should pause before we leap to judgement on others (and equally on ourselves). Are we sometimes too gentle, are we sometimes too harsh – perhaps we should pause before we too swiftly affirm or condemn?

> *(We may recall Gandalf, reminding Frodo,*
> *who is wondering if Gollum should die, -*
> *Deserves it! I daresay he does. Many that live*
> *deserve death. And some that die deserve life.*
> *Can you give it to them? Then do not be too*
> *eager to deal out death in judgement. For even*
> *the very wise cannot see all ends.[5])*

---

5   "The Lord of the Rings", J. R. R. Tolkien, first volume
         published in 1954. Allen & Unwin

Amos continues, announcing that God is saying:

> *I hate, I despise your religious festivals; your assemblies are a stench to me. Even though you bring me burnt offerings and grain offerings, I will not accept them. Though you bring choice fellowship offerings, I will have no regard for them. Away with the noise of your songs! I will not listen to the music of your harps. Let justice roll on like a river, righteousness like a never-failing stream!*

All the planning, all the cleaning, all the offerings, all the preparation, all the music – even those beautiful harps – are worth nothing. Because there is no justice. Amos has spelt out in previous words what has gone wrong:

> *There are those who hate the one who upholds justice in court and detest the one who tells the truth… You levy a straw tax on the poor and impose a tax on their grain. There are those who oppress the innocent and take bribes and deprive the poor of justice in the courts.*

The accusation is that here are people who oppress the poor, and who treat badly those who stand up for those poor. Here are people who use their wealth and power to keep down, not to build up. Perhaps it is not too fanciful to broaden the application to include any abuse of power: emotional, political, physical, spiritual or intellectual.

The oppression that worried the prophets was intentional and informed, sometimes vindictive. For those who oppress by accident there is no doubt much that can be learnt and changed, but intentional actors are the ones primarily in Amos' sights.

Martin Luther King quoted this passage in his 'I have a dream' speech.[6] The shepherd from Tekoa to the preacher from Alabama. Few of us will sit easy under these words, but the book of Amos is a call to repentance, not a condemnation without hope.

And the compilers of the writings of the Old Testament, mostly, historians have concluded, important and serious scholars and religious figures, no doubt responsible for carefully-crafted assemblies and ceremonies, ensured the words of Amos were recorded. That says a great deal about their integrity.

For reflection

- What can undermine our commitment to justice?

---

6   Speech given in Washington, 28 August 1963

— 15 —

Pausing, looking
and choosing

Stand at the crossroads
Jeremiah 6:16

Another phrase from a prophet, this time Jeremiah.

> *This is what the Lord says: "Stand at*
> *the crossroads and look; ask for the ancient*
> *paths, ask where the good way is, and walk in*
> *it, and you will find rest for your souls."*
> *But you said, "We will not walk in it."*

It is a common enough expression: 'I felt I was at a real crossroads' – one of those images that works across all cultures. Sometimes the choice does not particularly matter, the roads may join up at another point, but sometimes it does, and, for the prophet Jeremiah, this is one of those times. Real decisions have to be made, and one of the tests of wisdom is how these decisions are made.

The commands are specific:

They are to stand. This is not a moment to rush on, they can only stand if they have stopped.

They are to look. In their pausing there should be consideration, a looking around at how the world is.

They are to ask for the ancient paths. This is not always a popular thing to do. Have they the humility to realise that the old ways may have as much (or more) wisdom as the new?

They are to ask where the good way is. They are to be alert to what is right and wrong, and what will see them safely home.

And they are to walk in it. This is the path they must follow. It is not enough to think it, they need to do it. It is not enough to know the map well, they need to travel.

And then the promise – *You will find rest for your souls.*

Those five commands and the promise would perhaps cause much thought, and each one may have been picked up by different listeners round the circle. But there is then the firm rebuke: *But you said, "We will not walk in it."*

Jeremiah feels they have made their choice. Did he know through watching their actions or hearing their words? What caused them to decide not to walk in the right paths? The challenge is repeated in the next sentence:

I appointed watchmen over you and said, "Listen to the sound of the trumpet!" But you said, "We will not listen."

Just before the sentence about the crossroads Jeremiah highlights one of the failings of the leadership, of the prophets and priests:

> *They dress the wound of my people as though it were not serious. "Peace, peace," they say, when there is no peace. Are they ashamed of their detestable conduct? No, they have no shame at all; they do not even know how to blush.*

Here are people who seem to have lost reference points for which behaviours were helpful and which were not. They needed a reminder. And the sharp-eared would have noticed the echo of Wisdom calling in the book of Proverbs, *but you refused to listen.*

For reflection

- Is Jeremiah's advice helpful when we need to make decisions?

— 16 —

The strength of gentleness

A bruised reed he will not break
Isaiah 42:3

> *Here is my servant, whom I uphold, my chosen*
> *one in whom I delight; I will put my Spirit on*
> *him, and he will bring justice to the nations.*
> *He will not shout, or cry out, or raise his voice*
> *in the streets. A bruised reed he will not break*
> *and a smouldering wick he will not snuff*
> *out. In faithfulness he will bring forth justice;*
> *he will not falter or be discouraged till he*
> *establishes justice on earth.*

Perhaps some who were listening would not have wanted it to be noticed how much these words brought relief. The bruised reed was not going to be broken, great news indeed. Many of us know we are bruised, and we hold desperately to the hope that we will not be finally broken. And here this hope is affirmed and confirmed.

It may have felt unexpected in this context, because the passage is about justice. The bringer of righteous judgement is here; a potentially difficult conversation, to say the least. But we learn that his agenda is not to break the bruised reed, nor snuff out the smouldering wick. If we have ever felt fragile going into a potentially difficult conversation and then the other person treats us well and keeps us safe, then perhaps there is a faint echo of this promise about Christ.

The word 'justice' is often used in a very broad sense in Isaiah, as Barry Webb writes: *It is nothing less than to put God's plans for his people into full effect*[7]. Part of this plan is that the bruised reed will not be broken…

Here is a reminder that this is what Jesus, fulfilling the Isaiah prophecies, is like. We see it in his encounters with individuals, in the stories he told, and in his teaching:

> *Come to me, all you who are weary and burdened, and I will give you rest. Take my yoke upon you and learn from me, for I am gentle and humble in heart, and you will find rest for your souls. For my yoke is easy and my burden is light.*

And that it is fine to admit that we are bruised, or that sometimes the flame seems very weak and barely flickering. Part of this admission may be an honest questioning and awareness of what has bruised us, or of what caused the fire to fade.

We note the verse before – *he will not shout out*… some of us live in cultures which are

---

7   "The message of Isaiah" Barry Webb, 1996. IVP

currently quite shouty; here we are told that the promised Messiah who will change the world is not going to shout.

Or the verse after – *he will not falter or be discouraged* – Here is someone who will keep going to the end, and who will bring, and embody, encouragement.

There is wisdom in hearing the implicit challenge: we are called to receive this comfort but also to share it, to ensure that we are likewise careful not to break the bruised reeds, nor to extinguish the smouldering wicks. This is about justice to the nations. The gentleness is not only for our own circle; when we see a bruised reed among the strangers or our enemies, we are not to press onward to crush, that is not the way of the Messiah.

For reflection
- What is the place of gentleness in our words and actions?

— 17 —

Mercy matters

Love mercy
Micah 6:8

> *And what does the Lord require of you? To*
> *act justly and to love mercy and to walk*
> *humbly with your God.*

Much can be written on the first and last phrases of Micah's words, probably written in the early 8th Century BC, but perhaps one or two of the listeners focused on *Love mercy*. What might it look like to *love mercy*?

Perhaps it is to value and affirm those moments when others show mercy? Cheering our neighbours for their act of kindness, letting the child know that we noticed when she was kind.

Perhaps something about learning to receive mercy graciously? We can sometimes be tempted to think that we have no need for another's mercy, or shy away from admitting this need because we do not want to admit to being vulnerable; neither position is very healthy.

What might it mean to develop our habits so that our instinct is to be merciful in our thoughts, words and actions? There may occasionally be times when we need to be robust about wrong-doing (we are indeed called to act justly) but we will still want to show compassion to the wrong-doer. Perhaps a helpful yet sobering guide is this: if we occasionally sense people are slightly scared of us, is that really as it should be? What reputation do we have, are we known as people who love mercy?

To understand, and to be thankful, that mercy is at the heart of God are central to Christian thinking. Trusting that God is rich in mercy, as Paul writes to the Ephesians, keeps things in perspective. And, as the writer of Lamentations says, *His mercies are new, every morning*.

The Micah passage comes in the context of asking how we should approach God:

> *Shall I come before him with burnt offerings, with calves a year old? Will the Lord be pleased with thousands of rams, with ten thousand rivers of oil? Shall I offer my firstborn for my transgression, the fruit of my body for the sin of my soul? He has shown you, O mortal, what is good. And what does the Lord require of you? To act justly and to love mercy and to walk humbly with your God.*

The three-fold response that Micah seeks is outward-looking: we are to walk, to act, to love. The prophet gently points out that wealth, achievement, or self-destructive behaviour (sometimes from the best of intentions) are not what is required. No doubt the early listeners smiled at the happy exaggeration (ten thousand rivers is a lot of oil) but would have noted the subtle temptation to think we can earn God's favour, that surely he will listen to me if I achieve this, or punish myself like that. There is no point putting on our best jacket for church if we are unmerciful to a slower pedestrian on the pavement, or believe the worst of our neighbour in the next pew. There is no point being too hard on ourselves for real or imagined misdemeanours whilst forgetting that it is in the walking humbly with our God that we receive true forgiveness and acceptance.

For reflection

- What does it look like in our daily lives to be people who love mercy?

– 18 –

Don't disregard the small

Though you are small
Micah 5:2

It is from the small town that the saviour will come, writes the prophet Micah:

> But you, Bethlehem Ephrathah, though you
> are small among the clans of Judah, out of
> you will come for me one who will be ruler
> over Israel, whose origins are from of old, from
> ancient times.

Bethlehem was not insignificant in its heritage: Jacob's beloved wife Rachel was buried on the road to Bethlehem. In Judges 12 we read that "Ibzan of Bethlehem led Israel" and was buried there. Most of the story of Ruth is set in Bethlehem, and above all, it was great King David's hometown. But it was still a small city and by the time of Micah, the golden days were in the past.

It is a reminder that the small and the vulnerable have a heritage; they will have had golden days when life was good and they were honoured. For some, sadly, these days may seem to have been pitifully few and a long time distant, but they were there. The crushed person we see in front of us should be valued not only for what they are and what they might yet be, but also for what they have been. And of course it may be ourselves who feel Bethlehem-ish. We may feel small, whilst others seem to be growing larger. We may feel that the moments of honour have long since gone. Let us remember Bethlehem.

The Bethlehem theme (repeated in a myriad of ways through scripture) is a comfort but also brings a challenge to those from powerful and successful backgrounds. Jesus' disciples begin to grasp this when they are made to realise that being rich does not guarantee spiritual success;

> *"It is easier for a camel to go through the eye of a needle than for someone who is rich to enter the kingdom of God." When the disciples heard this, they were greatly astonished and asked, "Who then can be saved?"*

Jesus replies that it may seem impossible in our eyes, but the power of God is limitless. We note that Jesus emphasises the work of God in this; we are saved not because we are educated or rich or successful, but because of the grace of God. If we may stretch the analogy a little, we may need to work quite hard to ensure that our outward appearance as a great city does not stop us being honest about our inner Bethlehem.

Phrases from the Prophets

But perhaps it is the traditional point that would have struck the listener most clearly: Strength to change the world will be found in weak places. Several hundred years later this theme is to be one of the dominant conversations in the life of Christ, and will be seen as being a core part of wise understanding of the workings of God. Jesus spoke about a mustard seed of faith being enough and highlighted the need to receive the kingdom of God like a little child. Paul wrote about God's grace being sufficient, because His power is made perfect in weakness. In following centuries hymn writers were to muse much on this, Frank Houghton just one example:

> *Thou who wast rich beyond all splendour,*
> *all for love's sake becamest poor.*[8]

To be like Bethlehem, it is enough. The wise are alert to the working of God in the small places, even in the little town of Bethlehem. And thus to our next section…

For reflection

- What might it mean to us that Jesus was born in Bethlehem rather than Jerusalem or Rome?

---

8   "Thou who was rich, beyond all splendour" Frank
        Houghton. 1894-1972

Phrases from the
John the Baptist
Narrative

— 19 —

Voices can be set free

And he began to speak
Luke 1:64

We move forward several hundred years, and this is Zechariah, who had been struck dumb after not believing the angel's message about the future birth of a son. He is too old, he says. In his response, there are parallels with the ancient (even then) narrative of Abraham and Sarah, before the birth of Isaac. His response seems similar to that of Mary, sixth months later. but it seems Mary asks the question *How can this be?* in rather a different tone to Zechariah.

When the new baby is due to be named, his mother Elizabeth says 'John.' People are surprised but Zechariah confirms by writing, 'His name is John.' *Immediately his mouth was opened and his tongue set free, and he began to speak.*

Mark would later write about Jesus:

> *People were overwhelmed with amazement.*
> *"He has done everything well,"they said. "He*
> *even makes the deaf hear and the mute speak."*

Direct speech takes up a large proportion of the gospel narratives. Zechariah's initial words became a song of praise; is there something here about being set free to remember blessings, to be thankful and to be hope-filled? Is there something about being free to call out for mercy, forgiveness and new beginnings? Is there something about being enabled to be a voice for justice, compassion and peace? Zechariah's and Mary's songs, placed by Luke in his account almost side by side, have all these elements.

Is there something about the irrepressible response of people to good news?

- *The shepherds said to one another, "Let's go to Bethlehem and see this thing that has happened."*

- We read that on Palm Sunday *Some of the Pharisees in the crowd said to Jesus, "Teacher, rebuke your disciples!"* *"I tell you," he replied, "if they keep quiet, the stones will cry out."*

- A few days earlier we read: *As Jesus approached Jericho, a blind man was sitting by the roadside begging. When he heard the crowd going by, he asked what was happening. They told him, "Jesus of Nazareth is passing by." He called out, "Jesus, Son of David, have mercy on me!"*

> *Those who led the way rebuked him and
> told him to be quiet, but he shouted all the
> more, "Son of David, have mercy on me!"*

In some churches, prayers include the request
O Lord, open thou our lips.[9] Charles Wesley, who
knew that prayer well, was to write this line for
one of his hymns: *His praise, ye dumb, your loosened
tongues employ.*[10]

Some of us may be physically, emotionally
or spiritually mute; may Zechariah's experience
be an encouragement. *And he began to speak.*
The great narrative has begun, and there will be
a quiet emphasis on the voiceless finding their
voice. We know well enough from our world
that silencing dissent is always a disturbing sign
of over-controlling leadership. This has happened
throughout history, and we find a small but
significant example in Acts 4. Peter and John are
told by Caiaphas and his inner circle not to speak
or teach at all in the name of Jesus. And their reply
is simply: *"As for us, we cannot help speaking about
what we have seen and heard."*

Part of living wisely is ensuring that the voices
of the voiceless can be heard. In looking round
our circles of family, friends and colleagues, we
may note those whose contributions are often

---

9   The Book of Common Prayer 1662

10   O For a Thousand tongues to sing, Charles Wesley,
        1707-1788

squashed or unheard. We may smiling say "I couldn't get a word in edgeways" but if this happens too often, it may be worth exploring.

For reflection

- Whose are the voices we should encourage to be heard?

- Is our voice heard?

- Do we truly believe that God likes to hear our voice?

— 20 —

Unexpectedly attractive

Then went out to him…
Matthew 3:5

John the Baptist might not be the first choice for the welcoming team, among his opening remarks had been:

> *You brood of vipers! Who warned you to flee from the coming wrath?*

Yet, all these people went to see him…

> *Then went out to him Jerusalem and all Judea and all the region about the Jordan…*

There had been no prophet in Israel for four hundred years – sometimes called 'the silent years' – Many had said many things, but without that indefinable quality and authority that had marked out Amos or Hosea, Malachi, Micah or Isaiah, let alone Elijah… And then someone appeared, of priestly lineage, but in the desert. And the desert is a place with so many echoes in the people's narrative.

His message was uncompromising: "You need to repent."

It is not enough that you are the 'chosen people', something needs to change, and needs to be washed and renewed. It is all rather blunt and slightly offensive, and the crowds seem to love it and find it exciting. John continues: The anointed one, the Messiah, is about to start his ministry, if you think this is strong, see what he will say and do, I am only preparing the way.

To some it was too challenging, too personal, and the hope was lost in fear. Herod, Tetrarch of Galilee, son of the Herod who had conversed with the Magi, had been told by John that his marriage to Herodias was immoral. Herodias was icy in her fury: Herod imprisoned John, but we are equally told he found his conversation interesting. But when Herodias sees an opportunity, Herod falls into her trap (involving exploitation of her daughter) and has John killed.

This is the same Herod whom Pilate three years later wants to consider Jesus on a spring Friday morning in Jerusalem. Herod finds Jesus interesting, but again lacks courage, as he had with John, and does not do quite enough to save him (although some writers think that he was trying to send a silent message to Pilate by the way he dresses the prisoner before sending him back). Did Herod, deep down, want serious conversations with these two towering figures? Or did he not?

The crowds went out to him. Even Herod the Tetrarch was intrigued. Intellectual and spiritual hunger can be present in unexpected places, messages of truth have an inherent attraction. We may sometimes need particular courage to speak as we should (and discernment to check we are speaking for the sake of the wider good, not simply because we enjoy being offensive). We may equally need courage to receive challenging truth spoken to us.

For reflection

- Why is truth attractive?
- What can hold us back from hearing it as fully as we may need?

– 21 –

Often, the best question

> *What should we do?*
> *Luke 3:10*

Wisdom needs to have practical outworkings. The crowds by the River Jordan ask John the Baptist: "What should we do?"

> *John answered, "Anyone who has two shirts should share with the one who has none, and anyone who has food should do the same."*
> *Even tax collectors came to be baptised.*
> *"Teacher," they asked, "what should we do?"*
> *"Don't collect any more than you are required to," he told them.*
> *Then some soldiers asked him, "And what should we do?"*
> *He replied, "Don't extort money and don't accuse people falsely – be content with your pay."*

The question is asked by three different groups of people: the crowd; then, somewhat unexpectedly, the tax-collectors; then, even more surprisingly, the soldiers, who were Romans or mercenaries. There is no-one too unfashionable, too unpopular, too much on the wrong side to be drawn to John (and later to Jesus) — nobody is barred from asking this question. Did some in the crowd mutter "Who do these people think they are, that they claim a right to be involved, to ask questions?" Or were they so struck by John's unsubtle *You brood of vipers* that they were rightly worried about the state of their own souls and had lost any complacency?

John's answers to the thrice-asked question are specific and practical, focusing on generosity, care and not exploiting others. He focuses on specific behaviours, not the abstract, but the underlying theme forms the basis of any sound community: use power properly and well.

What should we do? Often, deep down we know, but we need a John the Baptist voice to spell it out. And if ever our search for wisdom appears distant from our daily lives, then we may wish to remember these exchanges.

For reflection

- If we were to ask this question to John the Baptist, what might he say to us?

Phrases from the
Jesus Narrative

— 22 —

Being willing to search

*Where is the one who has
been born king of the Jews?*
Matthew 2:2

It is the urgent and important question that ripples through the gospel accounts.

We move back three decades from the ministry of John the Baptist to the birth of Jesus.

*Where is the one who has been born king of
the Jews?*

It was a little tactless. Unsurprisingly, Herod *was disturbed* at this question and perhaps Matthew was rather understating the reaction. Herod was officially the king of the Jews, but he was not of David's line. And these outsiders had appeared and had asked the question which would undermine all his authority. He was indeed a little disturbed.

The Magi had seen the sign, knew what it meant, sensed their own yearning, but arrived in the wrong place (sometimes our journeying needs a little guiding, however wise we might be). They may have been guessing that Jerusalem, the capital, rich with history and, above all, the Temple, would be the birthplace. Or perhaps they thought that learned people would be there, who could help. They were distant travellers and may not have read the holy texts of these people; they may not have known the words of Micah that the local scholars knew. Revealingly and perhaps embarrassingly, Herod did not seem to know them either, he had to ask.

> When Herod had called together the chief
> priests and teachers of the law, he asked
> them where the Messiah was to be born. "In
> Bethlehem in Judea,"they replied, "for this
> is what the prophet has written: 'But you,
> Bethlehem, in the land of Judah, are by no
> means least among the rulers of Judah; for out
> of you will come a ruler who will shepherd my
> people Israel.'"

The word 'Shepherd' when linked to 'Ruler' is an echo of King David, and Bethlehem was David's city. The Magi had earlier asked a tactless question, and the scholars had now given Herod an even more tactless answer. This was unlikely to end well; Herod's response was to try and manipulate a violent end to the story.

Where is the one who has been born king of the Jews? There is a relentlessness in the searching. T S Eliot uses poetic licence to guess the feelings of the Magi after they had returned home:

> *We returned to our places, these Kingdoms,*
> *But no longer at ease here, in the old*
> *dispensation[11]*

Things were different, the old no longer satisfies. John Betjeman expresses the challenge and the wonder with a different but equally strong tone:

> *And is it true? And is it true,*
> *This most tremendous tale of all,*
> *Seen in a stained-glass window's hue,*
> *A Baby in an ox's stall?*
> *The Maker of the stars and sea*
> *Become a Child on earth for me?[12]*

Where is the one who has been born king of the Jews? The early listeners would have noted that this is the question being constantly asked, in different ways, throughout the gospel accounts; this is the one that the Magi – knowledgeable, philosophical, magical (in the ancient sense), and wise – were asking.

For reflection

- Why was, and is, the birth of Jesus so intriguing to so many?

- What might be the obstacles that may distract us from the search?

---

11   "Journey of the Magi" T S Eliot. 1888-1965

12   "Christmas" John Betjeman. 1906-1984

— 23 —

We can hold, we can carry

He took him up in his arms
Luke 2:28

There is an old chorus: 'He will hold me fast,'[13] and the thought of Christ holding us, protecting us, carrying us, is understandably of great comfort. But at this point in Luke's narrative, it is Christ who is being held:

> *Inspired by the Spirit, Simeon came into the temple; and when the parents brought in the child Jesus, to do for him according to the custom of the law, he took him up in his arms and blessed God.*

Luke thinks this moment is important enough to include it in the narrative of Simeon and Anna meeting Joseph and Mary in the Temple, shortly after Jesus is born. We often move swiftly to Simeon's moving prayer, known as the 'Nunc Dimittis' – 'Lord, now lettest Thou Thy servant depart in peace…' But perhaps the *took him up in his arms* has a significance in itself.

13   Ada Ruth Habershon. 1905

It is always an honour to hold a child or baby (or adult), and here is Simeon holding Jesus himself. Simeon is not a high priest nor a king, he has little religious or worldly status. He is faithful and patient, perhaps one of those people who always seem to be around and have the glint of hope in their eyes. And he is the one who holds the Christ-child.

Dare we say that whenever we hold someone else, in safe welcome and blessing, we are holding Christ? ("Whatever you are doing for the least of these, you are doing for me")

And may we, tentatively and with all humility, see in Simeon's attitude an example we can follow, that we are somehow called to 'hold' Christ, to do all we can to safeguard and honour him? Perhaps there are echoes when we feel awestruck when holding a baby, sensing that here is a miracle of life that is far beyond our making, that the welfare of this child profoundly and immeasurably matters. Whatever happens, I will not drop this child.

The story of Jesus' childhood is bound up with the mystery of the incarnation. The reactions to him in his early years are as significant as those in his adult ministry. 'Am I a Herod or a Simeon?' continues to be a key question: 'do I crush or do I hold?'

Simeon was not expecting this moment that day, or at least no more than any other; maybe he wondered, each morning, whether today would be the day. He had not put on special clothes nor undertaken special rituals. But in his wisdom he was ready, perhaps he was always ready, to hold the Christ-child.

For reflection

- In what ways do we 'hold Christ' in our lives?

— 24 —

Be cautious about
the high places

Led him to a high place
Luke 4:5

In Luke's account of Jesus in the wilderness, we read:

> *The devil led him up to a high place and showed him in an instant all the kingdoms of the world. And he said to him, "I will give you all their authority and splendour; it has been given to me, and I can give it to anyone I want to."*

Jesus has grown up and has been baptised by his cousin John, it has been a very public moment. John is the celebrity of the moment, but he draws attention to Jesus. And Jesus then disappears. He goes to the deep desert, where there is silence. And there he is tempted.

A high place: temptation can arrive when we are in a high place just as much as when we are down: success, status, a nice view, are not a defence.

Perhaps even the opposite: do we sometimes sadly have to think: 'They (or I) had so much, seemed to have all they might want or need – why was it all thrown away?'

It is a reminder to tread carefully if our path leads us over higher places, not to avoid them in themselves, but to be cautious, very cautious.

In an instant: a temptation can make our minds go into overdrive. Our imagination may tell us that if we just give in a little, then so many wonderful things will happen in an instant, all our problems will disappear. And we should beware that we can equally catastrophise in the other direction. Despair can similarly lead us astray: in an instant, we may be tempted to feel that every awful thing we can possibly imagine will arrive all at once.

Pausing, weighing up each thought or image, separating one by one, can be a helpful defence. *In an instant* may be a sign of over-promising, or of over-threatening. Wisdom will usually say: there is no rush.

> *It has been given to me, and I can give it to anyone I want to.*

It is the great lie at the heart of evil – 'If you follow me, then you will be given the satisfaction you desire.' Evil is inherently deceitful. When we are tempted into some action, it is not usually the action itself that attracts, but the feeling that we think the action will bring. Evil is incapable of producing the feelings of true satisfaction, joy or beauty that we desire. The very best it can do is create patchy, pale or twisted imitations that go sour very quickly. It is perhaps intentional and significant that the very first question in the Bible is the serpent's attempt to overturn truth...*Did God really say...?* Why do we trust the tempter's voice so often? It is not as if he has a great track record.

For reflection

- Why might the high places be as much a place of spiritual attack as the low places?

— 25 —

Hearing the silence

Jesus did not answer a word
Matthew 15:23

We are not told why. The context is this:

*Leaving that place, Jesus withdrew to the
region of Tyre and Sidon. A Canaanite woman
from that vicinity came to him, crying out,
"Lord, Son of David, have mercy on me! My
daughter is demon-possessed and suffering
terribly."*
*Jesus did not answer a word. So his disciples
came to him and urged him, "Send her away,
for she keeps crying out after us."*
*He answered, "I was sent only to the lost sheep
of Israel." The woman came and knelt before
him. "Lord, help me!" she said. He replied, "It
is not right to take the children's bread and toss
it to the dogs."*
*"Yes it is, Lord," she said. "Even the dogs eat
the crumbs that fall from their master's table."*
*Then Jesus said to her, "Woman, you have
great faith! Your request is granted." And her
daughter was healed at that moment.*

Jesus did not answer a word. It is a strange reaction, especially to someone in such need. Is this not the moment for an immediate kind response?

The response is going to come, and the daughter healed, but Jesus wants a conversation first, and silence may prompt one. What follows may sound like a harsh exchange to some ears, but clearly was not to the woman who responds robustly, swapping words on equal terms… and both seem rather to enjoy it. We note sadly that the disciples had simply wanted to send her away, perhaps Jesus' initial silence created a gap that they clumsily wanted to fill.

This is one of several occasions when Jesus uses a pause or a silence to slow down the narrative. The accusers of the woman caught in adultery are met initially with silence. There is a pause on the journey to Jairus' daughter. He is slow to move (two days!) on hearing that Lazarus is dying, and when he finally arrives, much too late, Mary and Martha both challenge him on his delay. He is silent when he is accused in front of Pilate.

The idea of God sometimes being silent appears in the Psalms, but the psalmists knew that this was not a sign that he was not listening. They and the New Testament writers understood that there is something significant about the God of all communication, about Christ the incarnate Word, deliberately sometimes not speaking.

Jesus did not answer a word: silence can be a powerful part of a conversation. Was Jesus pausing to allow the significance of the moment to sink in? Did he sometimes fall silent to provoke a reaction? Or to know that a pause would mean that the later blessings would be even more understood?

Whenever we feel God is silent, it is good to ask what this silence is teaching us about ourselves, and our levels of patience and trust. We do not always need to rush to fill the gaps.

For reflection

- What is the wise response when we feel that God is silent?

— 26 —

Hearing the affirmation

Well done
Matthew 25:21

In Matthew chapter 25 Jesus tells three stories about being ready, the middle one is often called 'The Parable of the Talents.' A master, before going on a journey, entrusts different amounts of gold to three servants. On his return, he rewards those who have made the most of what was entrusted to them, and is less than enthusiastic to the one who has simply hidden the gift. The first story is about being expectant for the master's return, the third is the reminder that when we are kind or unkind to others, especially to those in need, we are being kind or unkind to Christ.

There is much that can be said about the three stories and what they teach about readiness, accountability and the end of our lives, but perhaps one or two of the early listeners may have simply landed on this phrase in the middle one: *Well done, good and faithful servant.*

These words are given at the end of the parable, when all is made right, but Jesus had much earlier reminded his listeners that encouragement can be heard in the now as well as the future: *Blessed are the merciful, blessed are the peacemakers*, and the present tense would have been noted. Thus we may dare to imagine:

- Perhaps today someone has tried to show patience or forgiveness, courage or obedience – *Well done, good and faithful servant.*

- Perhaps someone has tried to hold on to hope and steadfastness – *Well done, good and faithful servant.*

- Perhaps someone has tried to be honest and kind or has tried to resist a particular temptation – *Well done, good and faithful servant.*

For some it can feel quite difficult to hear these words; we have made mistakes, we feel we should have done more, and we can be in the habit of allowing negative memories to drown out the still small voice saying *well done*. We may find it difficult to feel we are forgiven, or to forgive ourselves, and therefore, as an inappropriate self-inflicted punishment, we won't hear praise.

The servants had not known when the master would return and needed to be both expectant and patient. Good, faithful and servant are all significant words. In the Greek, the word translated 'good' has connotations of fit for purpose, excellence, of doing the right thing. The word for 'faithful' implies trusting as well as persevering. The word translated 'servant' originally meant slave (but with the understanding that slaves in those days were often treated well and had better security of lifestyle than hired servants, hence the entrusting with gold) but, whether slave or servant, with the understanding that the gifts still belonged to the master. In growing the gifts, we are serving him, the greater good, not simply ourselves.

If there has been a moment today when we have used our gifts, whatever they might be, then may we be able humbly to hear the voice: *Well done, good and faithful servant.*

For reflection

- As we look back on the day, when might the angels have been cheering?

— 27 —

God is fair

―――――――――――――――――――――

Friend, I do thee no wrong
Matthew 20:13

Another short phrase from a parable that would
have had power for early listeners. This is the
Authorised Version translation of Matthew 20:13
and the context is the parable about the hiring
of workers in a vineyard. The labourers are hired
at different times of day, but all receive the same
reward. Those who have been working longest find
this difficult (as many of the listeners no doubt
likewise would have done). The owner responds
with this phrase *Friend I do thee no wrong* and
explains his right to give to everyone equally.

The theological point of the story is that
we are not 'less saved' if we turn to God late in
life, and there were, and are, some listeners who
found this challenging – they had been part of
the community of faith all their lives, and these
newcomers were being treated with equal respect

and honour, hasn't anyone noticed how faithful I've been? There are echoes of the older brother's grumbles in the story of the Prodigal Son.

But there is this response: *Friend, I do thee no wrong.* You may think I have done wrong, but I have not. There is a calm and absolute authority here. God does not do us wrong, however we may be seeing the situation. He completely understands both our faithfulness and our failings. He loves us as we are.

The aggrieved long-term labourers in the vineyard had begun to grumble. Sometimes when we feel the world is against us, sometimes when we have been treated unfairly, we may ask: why is God treating me like this, why is this being allowed to happen?

The words take the question to a different context: the nature and motives of the landowner. The listeners would have noted the use of the word *friend* (or equally, in the Greek, *comrade*). This would have been unexpected; these are only hired labourers but are being addressed with respect and affection.

And then the simple *I do thee no wrong.* Whatever we may be going through, however unjust the situation may feel, this is a God who does us no wrong. Abraham has affirmed this belief in a holy and just God centuries before: *Will not the Judge of all the earth do right?* In ancient cultures deities were not always holy, to say the least. The great theme of the Old Testament is that this God is one, is holy, and is loving, so when he looks at the labourers in the story, he says *Friend, I do you no wrong*.

Those who grumbled perhaps had found it difficult to remember to be thankful for what they had been given, and had fallen into the trap of worrying too much about what others had been given.

For reflection

- What difference might it make to our experience of unexpected and inexplicable challenges to have in mind this phrase: *Friend, I do thee no wrong?*

— 28 —

Power in action

The phrase 'spoke up' does not quite capture it. When Caiaphas says something, then this is to be the direction of travel. He is used to exercising power to solve problems and stay in control. When he speaks up, the council and Jerusalem take note, and nod obediently.

> *Then one of them, named Caiaphas, who was high priest that year, spoke up, "You know nothing at all! You do not realise that it is better for you that one man die for the people than that the whole nation perish."*

This was not a reaction to the provocative donkey procession, nor to the offensive turning over the tables in the Temple, but was declared a few days earlier, on hearing the news that people were saying that Jesus had brought Lazarus back from the dead. This is the context:

> *Some of them went to the Pharisees and told them what Jesus had done. Then the chief*

priests and the Pharisees called a meeting of
the Sanhedrin. "What are we accomplishing?"
they asked. "Here is this man performing many
signs. If we let him go on like this, everyone
will believe in him, and then the Romans will
come and take away both our temple and our
nation."

The fear is palpable, and Caiaphas decides that Jesus must go, and especially if he dares to come to Jerusalem during Passover, with the Romans watching, Pilate in town, crowds gathering. It is unthinkable that the unpredictable northern preacher be allowed to stir things up.

There were three specific problems for Caiaphas, a skilled political survivor who got on well enough with Pilate to serve as High Priest through the whole of his governorship. First, the possibility of a riot with Jesus' talk of freedom (and it would not be terribly helpful if at the same time anyone was using a phrase like 'Son of David', the last thing we need is a royal claim...). Second, Jesus' teachings and actions: his attitude to the 'unclean' and to gentiles called into question the complex and lucrative systems surrounding the Temple. The Temple was by far the most important place and business in Jerusalem; spiritual significance aside, Caiaphas' own wealth (and his family's) derived from it.

The third issue was the blasphemous claims of Jesus. He is claiming to do what only God does.

And was saying things such as *Before Abraham was, I am* – putting himself outside linear time and appropriating the divine name; he was claiming he could forgive the sins of a paralysed man lowered through the ceiling; he was speaking about being the water of life to a Samaritan woman. All utterly unacceptable. Whatever Caiaphas' other motives may have been, he no doubt took his religion seriously, and Jesus pressed too many wrong buttons.

We do not know whether Caiaphas was already thinking about the morality of the means he would need to achieve his end. How could Jesus die without some lying and killing on the way? Two of the Ten Commandments are already looking somewhat vulnerable, and he is the High Priest. Perhaps the contradiction did not trouble him too much; occasionally, powerful people do not think that the rules apply to them. (There is a nice touch on Good Friday when the religious authorities pretend to be desperate not to break ceremonial regulations in their efforts to have Jesus convicted by a gentile, whilst simultaneously breaking much more sacred and deeper laws.)

It can be a common temptation, the end looks so attractive, and so necessary, that any means will do.

The next week would be difficult and uncertain, but they got through and all seemed sorted by Sabbath-time on Friday evening. Caiaphas perhaps slept well that night. But the Sunday after that, not quite so well...?

As we ponder wisdom, we may remember that something is not automatically right or just simply because a Caiaphas says it.

For reflection

- Who now have the powerful voices in our circles and in our society?

- How do we weigh their judgement?

- Do we ever use our own voices inappropriately powerfully?

— 29 —

The net is not
going to break

The net was not torn
John 21:11

Almost at the end of the scroll, the reader begins the final section of John's gospel.

> *Simon Peter, Thomas called the Twin, Nathan'a-el of Cana in Galilee, the sons of Zeb'edee, and two others of his disciples were together. Simon Peter said to them, "I am going fishing." They said to him, "We will go with you." They went out and got into the boat; but that night they caught nothing.*
>
> *Just as day was breaking, Jesus stood on the beach; yet the disciples did not know that it was Jesus. Jesus said to them, "Children, have you any fish?" They answered him, "No." He said to them, "Cast the net on the right side of the boat, and you will find some." So they cast it, and now they were not able to haul it in, for the quantity of fish. That disciple whom Jesus loved said to Peter, "It is the Lord!" When*

Simon Peter heard that it was the Lord, he put on his clothes, for he was stripped for work, and sprang into the sea. But the other disciples came in the boat, dragging the net full of fish, for they were not far from the land, but about a hundred yards off.

When they got out on land, they saw a charcoal fire there, with fish lying on it, and bread. Jesus said to them, "Bring some of the fish that you have just caught." So Simon Peter went aboard and hauled the net ashore, full of large fish, a hundred and fifty-three of them; and although there were so many, the net was not torn. Jesus said to them, "Come and have breakfast."

The minds of the attentive circle may have stayed on any number of phrases and echoes (Were there smiles at Peter's hurried remembering of his clothes only to get them soaked a moment later? Why so long to recognise Jesus? Musings at bread and fish being mentioned again, as if recalling that child on the hillside: what would it feel like to be invited to breakfast on the beach by Jesus? Is 153 significant or simply a number?) but here we will note just one.

The net was not torn: why does John want to tell us that the net does not break?

In the confusion, thrill and uncertainty after the Resurrection, Peter decides to go back to what he knows best, he goes fishing. His friends are supportive: *We will go with you.* They catch nothing. We do not know if they reacted to this disappointment with frustration or the customary patience of fishermen. Given everything, one would have thought that some fish would indeed have been an encouragement; just this once, a break would be nice. But it was not to be.

Does the voice from the shore rub salt into the wound, asking the unnecessary question? Or does it land well, showing compassion and interest (and the word 'children' is interesting). They answer simply "No." We do not know their tone of voice. Then the encouragement to try one more time, to cast the net again. They do so, perhaps with the eternal optimism of fishermen, or out of obedience, or from wanting the voice to be quiet. One last time, on the other side. One last time.

The catch is enormous. The number is big and the fish are large (There is no such thing as a small fish in the church of God). And then John makes a point of telling us that the net does not break. An unnecessary detail perhaps, but Luke has gone out of his way to note at a similar event at the beginning of Jesus' ministry that on that occasion the nets began to break (Luke 5,6). This time, post-resurrection, the net holds.

There may come a time when our lives seem too full, there may come a time when we are not sure how everything we value will be brought safely home. Or perhaps we are nervous about growing our horizons, being stretched in new ways and facing new challenges. The Easter narrative says that the net is not going to break. All that is entrusted to, and given by, Christ will be held safe.

As the early church got underway, growing and spreading quickly, persecuted ruthlessly, full of robust discussions and sad martyrdoms, a speedy multiplication of people much larger than 153, perhaps one or two looked back to that spring morning by the sea of Galilee, and remembered that the net did not break.

For reflection

- In our lives, where are we nervous that the net might break?

- Is this passage reassuring, or is the author reading too much into a simple phrase?

Phrases from the Life of the Early Church

— 30 —

Sharing the thinking

Discussing Together
Luke 24:15

*Now that same day two of them were going
to a village called Emmaus, about seven miles
from Jerusalem. They were talking with each
other about everything that had happened.
As they talked and discussed these things with
each other, Jesus himself came up and walked
along with them; but they were kept from
recognising him. He asked them, "What are
you discussing together as you walk along?"
They stood still, their faces downcast.*

What follows is a study of the Old Testament,
the offer of hospitality and a shared meal, and the
recognition that Jesus himself is with them. All of
these are significant but it seems that Luke wishes
first to emphasise one particular feature: He notes
they were talking with each other, discussing
things with each other, that Jesus asks what they
were discussing together. It is brought to the
reader's attention that this is a shared conversation,
a shared journey.

The point is being made that those who seek wisdom know the value of the *together*. It is a skill to be able to discuss together. Just occasionally there are 'discussions' which are not discussions at all, but one person deciding to tell everyone else what they should be thinking. Luke's repetition of *together* and *each other* implies a genuine shared search for understanding. This was a community of learning.

It is rather a typical Jesus moment to ask what is on their minds, despite already knowing. He wants them to explain to a third party, to sum up for a new listener, so that their thoughts are clarified. If ever our confusion is such that it feels difficult to disentangle, the request to articulate can be both challenging and important.

We are told that they were downcast. For some, a feeling of despair can lead to a wishing to travel alone, but these companions felt able to share the sadness and shock of what they were experiencing. They were willing to listen, whereas occasionally in our sadness we may not even want to hear anything else. Their desire to keep working things through led them to press their new companion to stay. In their sadness they were still looking for a way forward, and this hope and hospitality opened the door to a new chapter.

The meeting with the two disciples on the way to Emmaus has often been visited by artists, perhaps most notably by Caravaggio. The 'what it looked like' is indeed worth imagining, but equally it is important to honour, and to be intrigued by, the fact it happened at all; honesty, togetherness, welcome and listening were all part of the wisdom shown in this journey.

For reflection

- With whom are we walking as we ponder the deep questions?

— 30 —

Hearing the "No"

The spirit of Jesus
would not allow them
Acts 16:8

How does it feel when it is a 'NO'?

Were there times when Theophilus, patiently reading through Luke's account of the activities of the early church in Acts, wondered if his friend had missed out a line? What would he (and countless commentators since) have given for a word or two of explanation after the simple assertion:

> When they came to the border of Mysia, they tried to enter Bithynia, but the Spirit of Jesus would not allow them to.

Those of us who struggle with guidance find this tantalising. How did they know? Was it circumstances, a voice from heaven, a consensus after animated discussion, a strong feeling? Luke, please could you explain just a little more?

And Luke does not say, in much the same way he does not say what Jesus said to Zacchaeus in that transformative conversation in Jericho. Nor does he say if Paul and his companions were troubled or surprised by this 'NO'. The fuller passage, Acts 16:6-10, reads:

> Paul and his companions travelled throughout the region of Phrygia and Galatia, having been kept by the Holy Spirit from preaching the word in the province of Asia. When they came to the border of Mysia, they tried to enter Bithynia, but the Spirit of Jesus would not allow them to. So they passed by Mysia and went down to Troas. During the night Paul had a vision of a man of Macedonia standing and begging him, "Come over to Macedonia and help us." After Paul had seen the vision, we got ready at once to leave for Macedonia, concluding that God had called us to preach the gospel to them.

We note that the 'NO' was a second one, which can feel deflating, especially so soon after the first; but they do not give up. And then Paul has a vision, wakes his companions, and says: "We are going to Macedonia."

And they go. Did any ask why one late-night dream is a 'YES' when other inviting scenarios had produced a 'NO'? The implication is that they indeed did discuss it, even if the getting ready was 'at once.' A very literal translation of the word expressed as 'concluding' is 'together-stepping' – rather a good way of describing a shared decision to move.

The doors to Bithynia and indeed the Province of Asia had been closed. The door to Macedonia and thus Greece was open. Luke's inclusion of the 'NO' as well as the 'YES' reminds us that both responses are normal, and the outcome was positive: Paul's ministry in Greece, and his later letters to the churches there, have had enormous significance.

And perhaps those early listeners learnt the wisdom of being gentle on those, including themselves, who had faced a 'NO', and who needed patience and trust in the waiting for the 'YES'.

For reflection

- What helps us cope sensibly when we see an opportunity, but the answer is 'NO'?

— 31 —

Aiming high

If anything is excellent
Philippians 4:8

Finally... one can imagine the listeners in
Philippi, noticing the scroll was nearly finished,
hearing the word 'finally', leaning forward with
anticipation. They had heard a short letter read,
no doubt pondered the inspiring testimony and
rich theology therein. And now Paul is signalling
it is drawing to an end – how will he finish? Some
great exhortation for action? Some emotional
rallying cry?

It is neither of these things. Paul wants them to
fill their minds with goodness, quality, and beauty.

> *Finally, brothers and sisters, whatever is*
> *true, whatever is noble, whatever is right,*
> *whatever is pure, whatever is lovely, whatever*
> *is admirable – if anything is excellent or*
> *praiseworthy – think about such things.*

A friend once wrote out this verse on a label
and stuck it on his laptop. It helped him with
his internet searches. A twelve-year old used

to read it out each morning before he went to school. Both (and countless others) have found it transformative.

Paul has a high opinion of our ability to choose what we think about (James in his letter makes a similar point about our choice of words). This call for intentionality echoes Lamentations 3:21: *Yet this I call to mind and therefore I have hope: Because of the Lord's great love we are not consumed, for his compassions never fail.*

We sometimes spend time thinking about what we say and what we do; Paul would wish us to reflect equally on what we think, what we watch and hear. He goes on:

> *Whatever you have learned or received or heard from me or seen in me – put it into practice. And the God of peace will be with you.*

Is this boastful or is Paul reaching for anything that might help, and throwing self-deprecating restraint aside? He is writing from prison to distant friends, and if there is anything they can learn from him about faith and values, then he wants them to keep remembering.

This is perhaps not a sentence that many of us would dare to use, but it is useful in reminding that there is much we can learn from others – let's choose our role models well. And it may also challenge us to consider what are the parts of our lives which we would be content for people to see as good examples to follow. There is wisdom in checking what is going on in our minds, in learning to be self-aware, in being willing to self-examine.

> *Whatever is true, whatever is noble, whatever is right, whatever is pure, whatever is lovely, whatever is admirable – if anything is excellent or praiseworthy – think about such things.*

And, as with many preachers and writers, Paul's 'finally' is not quite the last thing he wants to say, but that can be for another time.

For reflection

- How do we best fill our minds with good things?

— 33 —

Avoid unnecessary quarrels

Chloe's household
1 Corinthians 1:11

Paul's opening to his letter to the Corinthians is slightly less fulsome than some of his other greetings. He is indeed thankful that they have been given many gifts:

> *I always thank my God for you because of his grace given you in Christ Jesus. For in him you have been enriched in every way – with all kinds of speech and with all knowledge.*

But does not comment on how these gifts have been used. He immediately moves on to what he has heard:

> *My brothers and sisters, some from Chloe's household have informed me that there are quarrels among you.*

Slight nervousness among the listeners... Were any from Chloe's household sitting round the room as Paul's scroll was read out? Had they been expecting their concern to be made public or was there now some embarrassment? (We could consider this theme at length: Whenever we make a complaint, how prepared are we for all parties to know? What may our motives truly be? What do we hope or expect to happen? And how do we respond when someone expresses concern to us about someone else? And how do we feel when we hear someone has complained about us?)

For Paul, a concern raised was not only a problem to be solved but an opportunity for teaching.

It seems that the quarrels came between different factions who were each following their own heroes, in modern language, it was all getting rather tribal. Paul does not want to be put on a pedestal, nor should anyone else:

> *For when one says, "I follow Paul," and another, "I follow Apollos," are you not mere human beings? What, after all, is Apollos? And what is Paul? Only servants, through whom you came to believe — as the Lord has assigned to each his task. I planted the seed, Apollos watered it, but God has been making it grow.*

Paul perhaps would have approved of the words of the great 18th-century preacher Jonathan Edwards, who talked about our attitude towards those we honour and value:

> *These are but scattered beams; but God is the*
> *sun. These are but streams; but God is the*
> *fountain. These are but drops, but God is the*
> *ocean.*[14]

To which we might add: it is because these good things are from God, the beams from the sun, the streams from the fountain, that they have such special lustre. We can both honour them and honour the source of all that is good in them.

As the letter unfolds, Paul responds to the disunity by talking about sharing the Lord's Supper properly, treasuring each other's gifts, the blessing of the Holy Spirit, and knowing that we are all members of the same body. He will write about the absolute priority of love.

And at least partly, perhaps largely, this is because someone in Chloe's household felt that Paul needed to know what was going on. May all the concerns we share or receive be used to such good effect, sometimes things just need to be said.

For reflection

- What causes the quarrels in the circles we frequent?

---

14   Jonathan Edwards, The Works of Jonathan Edwards, Vol. 17: Sermons and Discourses, 1730-1733

– 34 –

Avoiding only being a noise

A clanging cymbal
1 Corinthians 13:1

This 13th chapter of Paul's first letter to the
Corinthians is understandably and appropriately
often used in weddings and funerals. The
thoughtful description of love in the middle, the
vision of future clarity and wholeness at the end,
are found by many to be moving and inspiring.
But it is the opening paragraph that carries
the bluntest challenge, and Paul is writing to
discomfort his readers.

There was something about the Corinthians'
attitude to one another that troubled him, that
needed addressing. All their activities (remarkably,
even their almsgiving, or apparent willingness to
face martyrdom) eventually will count for nothing
for their eternal soul if the motives are about self-
aggrandisement rather than love.

If I speak in the tongues of men or of angels,
but do not have love, I am only a resounding
gong or a clanging cymbal. If I have the gift

*of prophecy and can fathom all mysteries and
all knowledge, and if I have a faith that can
move mountains, but do not have love, I am
nothing. If I give all I possess to the poor and
give over my body to hardship that I may
boast, but do not have love, I gain nothing.*

Perhaps Paul chooses the image of a clanging cymbal to indicate something that is noisy, irritating, out of place and distracting. A speaker may be thinking that their eloquence is marvellous and helpful. They may be loving the sound of their own voice, but that would seem to be the only thing they are loving – it is all rather painful. The Greek word translated 'clanging' could be translated 'screaming'.

The achievements in these opening verses are rightly held in high esteem. Paul does not say they should not be, but rather is saying that the person is not in such a state of grace as they may think (perhaps there is an echo of Jesus' sad comment in the Sermon on the Mount about those who give alms or pray loudly just so they can be seen to do so: They have had all the reward they are going to get).

But there are some who may need reassuring, who are in fact kinder than they think they are, and should not be over-scared by Paul's words: if we give a sandwich to someone in need, with a mix of frustration and uncertainty, but still somehow hoping the sandwich may be of some value, then perhaps we are more loving than we think, because at least part of the focus is their welfare. We want the best for them, even if we are unsure how best to help. A mustard seed of love is infinitely better than no love at all.

Paul's following words explain what this mustard seed looks like, and what it will continue to grow to be:

> *Love is patient, love is kind. It does not envy,*
> *it does not boast, it is not proud. It does*
> *not dishonour others, it is not self-seeking,*
> *it is not easily angered, it keeps no record*
> *of wrongs. Love does not delight in evil but*
> *rejoices with the truth. It always protects,*
> *always trusts, always hopes, always perseveres.*

Leave off the boasting and selfishness, the competitiveness and resentment, says Paul, and let the love keep growing. Because anything done in love is of God, it is permanent and will never end.

For reflection

- What does it look (or sound) like to love well?

- Why might Paul be so keen to stress its centrality?

— 35 —
We need all the help we can get

May have power
Ephesians 3:18

This prayer from Paul's letter to the Ephesians is rightly used to remind us of the immeasurable love of Christ, but the word *power* may equally have stuck in people's minds.

> *And I pray that you, being rooted and*
> *established in love, may have power, together*
> *with all the Lord's holy people, to grasp how*
> *wide and long and high and deep is the love*
> *of Christ, and to know this love that surpasses*
> *knowledge – that you may be filled to the*
> *measure of all the fullness of God.*

One could have imagined Paul simply praying for the Ephesians to grasp how wide and long is this love, but he takes a step back, praying that they would have *power* to grasp how wide and long. Why does he feel this is necessary?

Power is needed when there are obstacles to be overcome. Perhaps there are hinderances to us grasping the love of Christ and these need to be carefully dismantled or simply swept aside. Perhaps our hands are grasping onto something less helpful, and the fingers need to be prised away so that we can take hold of something better. Perhaps there are understandable reasons from events in the past and present which make it difficult to feel free to be loved, and power is needed to set us free.

It is comforting that we can pray for this power, it does not all depend on us. Kipling may write:

> *If you can force your heart and nerve and sinew*
> *To serve your turn long after they are gone,*
> *And so hold on when there is nothing in you*
> *Except the Will which says to them: 'Hold on!'* [15]

But sometimes the will is not quite strong enough and some outside help is very welcome. Even at our weakest we can still pray 'help'. We may feel that we cannot hold on, but we can pray to the God who will hold us.

Connected with this comfort is a challenge. If we never feel we need divine help, then perhaps it is not divine work we are doing. If all is to be done in our own strength, then it is unlikely we are truly building the kingdom of God. If we think we can do it all by ourselves, then what we are doing will not last for eternity after all.

We may need to rethink the feelings and impressions we have when we think of the word 'power.' It can feel an assertive or aggressive word,

---

15   "If" Rudyard Kipling, 1910

and thoughts of noise and overbearing style may come to mind. We can be distracted from remembering that the power of God is in the still small voice, pretending we can only see it in the earthquake, wind and fire.

Paul would want his listeners to know that much in our lives (ultimately, everything) needs divine power at work. And that this can be part of our prayers.

For reflection

- What are the blockages that can stop people knowing they are loved?

- How might Paul's use of the word 'power' help us in our understanding of wisdom?

— 36 —

Knowing your enemy

Like a roaring lion
1 Peter 5:8

Spiritual warfare is often referenced in the Bible, and, as in all warfare, it is vital to know one's enemies, to study their character and aims with due wisdom. Peter writes:

> *Be alert and of sober mind. Your enemy the*
> *devil prowls around like a roaring lion looking*
> *for someone to devour. Resist him, standing*
> *firm in the faith.*

The devil, the embodiment of evil, is compared to a fierce and destructive lion. And is searching, hunting out the least defended. But he can be resisted. Lions prefer to target those on the edge of the herd, or those already vulnerable. In this context, this is not those who are emotionally vulnerable – we are all thus – but those who are morally and spiritually ill-defended.

Elsewhere, the devil is portrayed differently. In Genesis the image is a snake

> *Now the snake was more crafty than any of the*
> *wild animals the Lord God had made. He said*
> *to the woman, "Did God really say...?"*

It is the first question in the Bible and apparently sounds neutral. Here temptation is cunning and beguiling, claiming to be in our best interests, wanting us to think we know best. A different approach from that of a prowling lion.

Elsewhere in the Bible another image is *Satan*, the adversary or accuser. It could be argued that some of the devil's most effective work is done by falsely bringing us down, by relentlessly accusing us.

For the early readers of St Peter, they would have noticed the hope. Peter feels that this lion can be resisted. James writes likewise *Resist the devil, and he will flee from you*. Occasionally we may feel that the threat or temptation of evil is so overwhelming that we might as well give in quickly. The New Testament writers see it differently, yes, the lion is dangerous, but it can be seen off. The image of "standing firm" is likewise used by Paul.

> *Therefore put on the full armour of God, so*
> *that when the day of evil comes, you may be*
> *able to stand your ground, and after you have*
> *done everything, to stand.*

Those round the campfire listening for wisdom will have noted that the Biblical writers constantly hold this balance. We are to be cautious and wary of evil – it can all too easily trick, devour, and accuse. But it is on the losing side, it can be resisted. In the drama of Revelation chapter 12, we read:

> *Then war broke out in heaven. Michael and his angels fought against the dragon, and the dragon and his angels fought back. But he was not strong enough, and they lost their place in heaven. The great dragon was hurled down – that ancient snake called the devil, or Satan, who leads the whole world astray.*

But he was not strong enough – that is the phrase we may need to remember if we are struggling with the presence of evil or of despair, whether close at hand or far away. Or of course the great Easter cry: Christ is risen; He is risen indeed, Alleluia. Pope John Paul II said in 1986: "We are an Easter people, and Alleluia is our song". It is a song that the dragon/lion/snake/Satan does not like very much.

For reflection

- How well do we know our weaknesses when it comes to temptation?

- If we were to choose an image to personify evil, what would it be?

Phrases from the Drama to End All Drama

— 37 —

Trusting enough to
open the door

I stand at the door and knock
Revelation 3:20

The opening chapters of the book of Revelation remind the listener of the splendour and authority of Christ. He is the first and the last, he holds the seven stars, he is the one calling the church to account (and seeking to encourage) – and he is knocking. He is not bursting through the door. He is standing, waiting, to see if the door will be opened.

Perhaps there are echoes of Luke 12:35,36

> Be dressed ready for service and keep your
> lamps burning, like servants waiting for their
> master to return from a wedding banquet,
> so that when he comes and knocks they can
> immediately open the door for him.

Some of us may be thinking of the famous painting by Holman Hunt, 'The Light of the World'. He liked the theme so much that he painted it three times and one of his copies toured the globe. He paints the picture so there is no handle on the outside of the door, and enough weeds have grown to show that the door has not been opened for some time.

> *If anyone hears my voice and opens the door, I will come in and eat with that person, and they with me.*

There is a truth, a challenge and a promise. Jesus is not going to break down the door. His character is love, patience and humility, and so the door is not going to be forced.

And the challenge is whether we will open the door. Are we ready for what that might mean? C.S. Lewis writes:

> *Imagine yourself as a living house. God comes in to rebuild that house. At first, perhaps, you can understand what He is doing. He is getting the drains right and stopping the leaks in the roof and so on; you knew that those jobs needed doing and so you are not surprised.*

> *But presently He starts knocking the house about in a way that hurts abominably and does not seem to make any sense. What on earth is He up to? The explanation is that He is building quite a different house from the one you thought of – throwing out a new wing here, putting on an extra floor there, running up towers, making courtyards. You*

thought you were being made into a decent
little cottage: but He is building a palace.
He intends to come and live in it Himself.[16]

The promise is that, and we say it reverently: we will be friends, we will be family, as united and trusting as those who eat together. The bonds of fellowship through sharing a meal have been strong in all cultures, it is unsurprising that Jesus commanded us chose a meal as the great sign and expression of his love. Do this "in remembrance of me."

Perhaps the early listeners, gripped as this extraordinary vision is opened before them, may have pondered the loving patience of the Christ who knocks, their need to hear his voice and to open the door, however tentatively, and then the sense of honour and excitement – He wants to eat with me, they may have pondered, as he had with Zacchaeus, Mary and Martha, with the apostles themselves.

But sometimes we may be nervous about opening the door. Part of wisdom is knowing whom we can trust. This verse comes from the letter to the Laodiceans. It seems that they felt they were doing fine: moderate and careful, wealthy and well-clothed. But somewhere in their journey they had shut Jesus out – yet he carries on patiently knocking.

---

16   "Mere Christianity" C S Lewis, 1952, Geoffrey Bles

For reflection

- What would a meal with Jesus be like?

- How can anyone be assured that they are genuinely invited and no impostor at such a meeting?

— 38 —

The suffering of love
has eternal power

Looking as if it had been slain
Revelation 5:6

"Holy, holy, holy" we read in Revelation, chapter 4 – this is a Hebrew way of expressing a superlative.

In Revelation 5 we find this three-fold pattern used again:

Then I saw a Lamb, looking as if it had
been slain, standing at the centre of the throne,
encircled by the four living creatures and the
elders.

The description is repeated a few lines further,

You are worthy to take the scroll and to open
its seals, because you were slain, and with
your blood you purchased for God persons
from every tribe and language and people and
nation (…)

> *Worthy is the Lamb, who was slain, to receive*
> *power and wealth and wisdom and strength*
> *and honour and glory and praise!*

The word 'slain' can hardly be missed. In John's vision the centrality of the sacrificial love of Christ is not to be forgotten. (And, as often in the book of Revelation, this theme is not to be downplayed or subordinated to any desire to make the picture easy to visualise). There are echoes of Jesus' post-resurrection appearances. The disciples, including Thomas, had seen the wounds in his side and hands. Some commentators wonder whether, when Jesus held up bread to be blessed with the two travellers to Emmaus, the marks on his wrist were revealed as his sleeves slipped down. Amidst the wonder of the resurrection, the signs of the crucifixion remained.

There may be something here about reassurance. In the theology of the Old Testament the shedding of the life-blood of the sacrifice was seen as an essential part of the rituals of atonement. And so the vision emphasises and reminds that this was a real death, blood was shed, the readers could be assured that their sins truly are washed away. As Charles Wesley wrote on the first anniversary of his renewal of faith.

He breaks the power of cancell'd sin.
He sets the prisoner free;
His blood can make the foulest clean,
His blood avail'd for me [17]

In the context of the culture and background of John's readers, the reminder that the lamb had been slain would have been comforting, not gruesome. This is how much we are loved.

There may also be something about honouring suffering. The vision will indeed go on to include the words that "Death shall be no more, neither shall there be mourning nor crying nor pain any more" but that does not mean that the suffering did not matter.

The vision that John wished to pass on to the oppressed and scattered readership was pastoral as well as theological. He wished his readers to know that the reminder of the cost of the sacrificial love of redemption remains part of the glory of the risen and ascended Christ. As Matthew Bridges wrote, a century after Charles Wesley:

Crown Him the Lord of Love.
Behold His hands and side;
Rich wounds yet visible above,
in beauty glorified. [18]

---

17   "O for a Thousand Tongues" Charles Wesley, 1739

18   "Crown Him with Many Crowns" Matthew Bridges, 1851

Is it too much to believe that any small suffering from love that we may experience is somehow caught up in Christ's? That his suffering encompasses, and heals, ours? Whenever we are called to bear 'the wounds of love', in Oscar Wilde's phrase,[19] we can trust that they are known and honoured, that they are held in heaven.

For reflection

- "The suffering of love is honoured and remembered" – what difference might this sentence make to our lives?

---

19   "The Selfish Giant" Oscar Wilde, 1888

— 39 —

One day we will not
need to be afraid

There was no longer any sea
Revelation 21:1

John draws to a close the description of his vision; in the penultimate chapter we read:

> Then I saw a new heaven and a new earth, for the first heaven and the first earth had passed away, and there was no longer any sea. I saw the Holy City, the new Jerusalem, coming down out of heaven from God, prepared as a bride beautifully dressed for her husband. And I heard a loud voice from the throne saying, "Look! God's dwelling-place is now among the people, and he will dwell with them. They will be his people, and God himself will be with them and be their God. "He will wipe every tear from their eyes. There will be no more death" or mourning or crying or pain, for the old order of things has passed away."

> He who was seated on the throne said, "I am making everything new!"

In the midst of the cosmic and overarching assurances there is one phrase which perhaps might have caused a particular sigh of relief: There was no longer any sea.

The sea was, and is, a frightening place to many. Its power appears immeasurable and beneath its surface swim unknown mysteries and dangers. Monsters lurk there. We are perhaps at our most vulnerable, most helpless, in the sea. This does not detract from its beauty and attraction, but it was often used in the scriptures as a symbol of humanity's puniness. The Jewish nation did not have the nautical expertise and confidence of some other Mediterranean realms. The sea became the symbol of where fears find their home, where they are difficult to catch or see, and are moving and stirring, immeasurable and threatening.

There was no longer any sea. As those words were read aloud perhaps one or two minds would have leapt to deepest fears (the very word 'deepest' has echoes of the sea) and began to dare to believe that these fears truly would cease when all is brought together, when all is made new. Did the reader inject drama and joy into this simple sentence? Was it met with quiet exquisite relief, or cheers and embraces? Did he or she have to call them back to order so the next sentence about the Holy City could be heard?

In the Book of Common Prayer people are encouraged to pray for, and give thanks for, *remission of our sins, and all other benefits of his passion.* We rightly often emphasise the centrality of remission of our sins, forgiveness, when we talk about salvation, but the Greek word is broader still, meaning something like 'wholeness' or, to use modern terminology, 'complete well-being'. Revelation 21 reminds us that not only our sins and guilt are taken away but all our fears plus – as the passage continues – all our griefs and sorrows. All other benefits of his passion indeed.

Our deepest fears may often be private and personal, and to face up to them can be as challenging as it can be liberating (and sometimes needs careful help). Perhaps this brief phrase was enough to help one or two of the listeners to begin a journey of realising that their fears will not last forever, to know the darkness of the valley is short, and they will emerge into the sunlight before too long. The walk through the valley is then so much easier to face.

John does not explain, he simply says it. And perhaps knew that for the fearful, this was the phrase they longed to hear. *There was no longer any sea.*

For reflection

- Of what are we most scared?

- How may we develop some assurance that our deepest fears will one day disappear?

— 40 —

We cannot describe
everything

On each side of the river
stood the tree of life
Revelation 22:2

The listeners may have been perplexed; they have been asked to visualise so many extraordinary images in this vision, and now this. Despite noble efforts of artists through the centuries it is difficult to picture one tree standing on both sides of the bank of a river.

Perhaps it is a reminder that truth is sometimes inexpressible in our usual words. If ever we struggle to wrap up a belief or experience in a neat, closed paragraph, then this might be a healthy sign: we need not worry if we cannot describe it all in one go. It helps to keep us humble, especially if we live in a culture that highlights what can be articulated or enumerated.

There is also a sense of threads being pulled together. In Ezekiel 47:12 we read

> *Fruit trees of all kinds will grow on both banks*
> *of the river. Their leaves will not wither, nor*
> *will their fruit fail. Every month they will bear*
> *fruit, because the water from the sanctuary*
> *flows to them. Their fruit will serve for food*
> *and their leaves for healing.*

The ancient vision is being subsumed in this new greater vision, and every life-giving tree is part of the tree of life itself, which is now restored to us. In the opening narrative of the Bible, humanity is separated from the tree of life, now we are in the garden once again. (It echoes Jesus' words to the penitent thief on the cross *Today you will be with me in paradise*, paradise being a word of Persian origin signifying beautiful gardens). Nothing that was truly good will ultimately be truly lost, quite the opposite, it will be restored, renewed and made even better than before, made complete.

The context is the opening of the final chapter of Revelation.

> *Then the angel showed me the river of the*
> *water of life, as clear as crystal, flowing from*
> *the throne of God and of the Lamb down the*
> *middle of the great street of the city. On each*
> *side of the river stood the tree of life, bearing*
> *twelve crops of fruit, yielding its fruit every*
> *month. And the leaves of the tree are for the*
> *healing of the nations.*

And here there will be healing, not just for one tribe, nor for only the scattered small groups of Christians hiding across the Roman Empire in fear of persecution, but for the nations. John was writing this whilst in exile on the prison island of Patmos. Even in those conditions, he is looking forward, up and out. And he is full of hope that is too big to be sensibly pictured, but that does not stop him. Indescribable, flowing, fruitful, restoring and healing life, too big for words, so big it is on both sides of the river.

The wise reader may have simply enjoyed the feeling, the artistry and the drama. Knowing the truth of the thinking behind this quotation, often attributed to Albert Einstein: *Not everything that can be counted counts, and not everything that counts can be counted.*

For reflection

- How does hope fit into our understanding of wisdom?

And Finally

— 41 —

Eyes open for the crumbs

Let nothing be wasted
John 6:12

"Gather the pieces that are left over, let nothing be wasted." Thus Jesus instructs his disciples at the end of the feeding of the five thousand.

This little book, with its slightly random selection of Bible phrases, could be seen as a scattering of crumbs. Readers may know of many other phrases that could have been chosen as we seek to build up a picture of a life lived wisely, how we might find counsel for the perils (and joys), small or large, that we face.

Among many other omissions we have not included one of the most obvious verses; *The fear of the Lord is the beginning of wisdom,* with its message that if our thoughts and behaviours are orientated to God, then they are likely to fall into place. Nor the opening verses of John's gospel, and the significance of Jesus as the Word, made flesh. Here is wisdom, walking the roads of Galilee, Samaria and Jerusalem. What does it look like?

And so this is a very inadequate book. The not-very-original theme is that wisdom can be found in many different places, in many unexpected corners of narratives. It takes attention to gather up the pieces, to search for fragments of nourishment amidst the stones and weeds of the paths we tread. We can be distracted by so many things.

At the beginning the definition was offered that wisdom is to do with understanding how the world is, and how to live well within it. It is not the same as cleverness, and it only comes with age if the aged have learnt from their experience. An alert child can be as wise as an unalert adult, but the adult has had more opportunity to observe and learn. To those to whom much has been given, much may be expected.

We will all have different ways of remembering, of noting from our experiences what is helpful to consider, and then how to keep this wisdom in a storehouse that can help resource us day by day. *Gather the pieces that are left over, let nothing be wasted;* To ensure that wisdom, noticed and gleaned in all sorts of contexts, is stored not wasted, some people write, draw or discuss with friends (conversations are often more memorable than individual unrecorded reflections, important though they are at the time). Some people paint or sing, or intentionally associate learning moments with particular places and times.

We began with Queen Esther, and the reminder that choices are to be made, wisdom to be exercised, in the time and place in which we find ourselves. We are where we are and we do what we can. In so doing, we play our part in the great story. May we seek to do so wisely, ever on the lookout to pick up crumbs of wisdom in all sorts of likely and unlikely places; perhaps even in our reflections over what is going on when people make lament for cucumbers.

Index of Old Testament Passages

Index of New Testament passages

Thematic view:

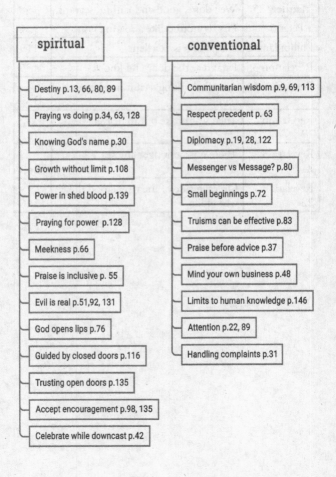

spiritual

- Destiny p.13, 66, 80, 89
- Praying vs doing p.34, 63, 128
- Knowing God's name p.30
- Growth without limit p.108
- Power in shed blood p.139
- Praying for power p.128
- Meekness p.66
- Praise is inclusive p. 55
- Evil is real p.51,92, 131
- God opens lips p.76
- Guided by closed doors p.116
- Trusting open doors p.135
- Accept encouragement p.98, 135
- Celebrate while downcast p.42

conventional

- Communitarian wisdom p.9, 69, 113
- Respect precedent p. 63
- Diplomacy p.19, 28, 122
- Messenger vs Message? p.80
- Small beginnings p.72
- Truisms can be effective p.83
- Praise before advice p.37
- Mind your own business p.48
- Limits to human knowledge p.146
- Attention p.22, 89
- Handling complaints p.31

Wisdom in 4 Baskets

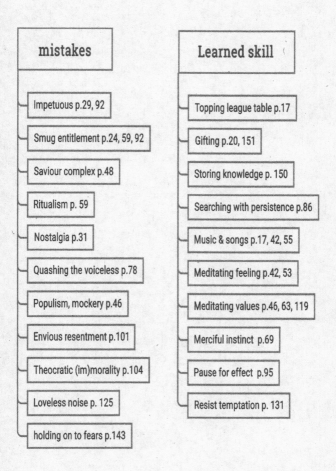

mistakes

Impetuous p.29, 92

Smug entitlement p.24, 59, 92

Saviour complex p.48

Ritualism p. 59

Nostalgia p.31

Quashing the voiceless p.78

Populism, mockery p.46

Envious resentment p.101

Theocratic (im)morality p.104

Loveless noise p. 125

holding on to fears p.143

Learned skill

Topping league table p.17

Gifting p.20, 151

Storing knowledge p. 150

Searching with persistence p.86

Music & songs p.17, 42, 55

Meditating feeling p.42, 53

Meditating values p.46, 63, 119

Merciful instinct p.69

Pause for effect p.95

Resist temptation p. 131